The Complete Guide to

Northern Gulf Seafood

The Complete Guide to
NORTHERN GULF SEAFOOD

BY TOM BAILEY

Photography by Celeste Ward

PELICAN PUBLISHING COMPANY
GRETNA 2013

The word "Pelican" and the depiction of a pelican are
trademarks of Pelican Publishing Company, Inc., and are
registered in the U.S. Patent and Trademark Office.

Library of Congress Cataloging-in-Publication Data

Bailey, Tom, 1947-
  The complete guide to Northern Gulf seafood / by Tom Bailey ; photography
by Celeste Ward.
    pages cm
  Includes index.
   ISBN 978-1-4556-1848-4 (hardcover : alk. paper) — ISBN 978-1-4556-1849-1
(e-book) 1. Cooking (Seafood) 2. Cooking, American. 3. Cooking—Mexico, Gulf
of, Region. I. Title.
  TX747.B26 2013
  641.6'92—dc23
                                                              2013012129

Printed in Singapore

Published by Pelican Publishing Company, Inc.
1000 Burmaster Street, Gretna, Louisiana 70053

Contents

Preface 7

Acknowledgments 11

Introduction: What's in the Gulf of Mexico? 13

Making Your Selection 17

Handling and Preserving 21

Fish Forms and Butchering 25

Basic Cooking Techniques 35

Shellfish 39

Finfish 79

Index 191

Preface

To be perfectly clear, this is not a book of newly created seafood recipes.

Rather, this is a book about the fish and shellfish that come from northern gulf waters—fish that you might catch, find in a fresh market, or have a friend give to you—and ways to prepare each one based on flesh type, fat content, and types of cuts available with each species.

The first goal of this book is to target species-specific recipes and make sure that they are practical in their preparation and that their ingredients can be found in most grocery stores. Most importantly, by matching ingredients and cooking style with a specific seafood species, the resulting dish will provide a superior dining experience.

A second goal of this book is to help cooks overcome any anxiety of preparing seafood because it feels and looks different than pork, beef, or chicken. However, fish is a lot easier and usually a lot quicker to cook than other meats. In addition, it is a great vehicle for almost any type of dish or flavor that you want to achieve. It carries almost every herb and spice well, and few are the vegetables that don't make a wonderful accompanying dish. Like Italian? Sprinkle on the Italian spices. Greek? Creole? Chinese? Same thing. Sprinkle on what you like and to the degree of spiciness that you enjoy and you will have an enjoyable dish. Favoring citrus? Most fish are enhanced with orange, lemon, lime, and even tangerine. What about the holy trinity (celery, onions, and bell pepper)? It is almost impossible to have a bad fish dish with the addition of those three classic ingredients.

Further along in this book you will find recipes tied to specific species of fish, just to provide an extra measure of assurance that whatever species you have is well-tailored to a certain set of ingredients. It would be a shame, however,

to think that a recipe designed for triggerfish would not be good with anything else. In fact, except for tuna and, maybe, swordfish, every recipe in this book can be used successfully with every finfish species.

The third goal is to offer recipes that capture the cooking styles and flavors of the northern gulf region, ranging from Tampa Bay, Florida, to Mexico. The recipes in this book were chosen not only because they are delicious but also because they represent the cooking and presentation styles that are most enjoyed along this stretch of coast.

To do that, included in addition to our own recipes are superior recipes from resources all along the northern gulf (plus some from other places that have done an excellent job with seafood found in northern gulf waters). Some of the recipes came from fishermen and those who live along the coast and whose recipe development consists of throwing some good stuff together to result in wonderful dining experiences. Some of those recipes appear in this book. It is our effort to remain true to the recipe in as close to the form in which we received or found it; as a result, at times the wording may be a little unusual. My hope is that you will enjoy the differences in how different folks write and talk about the food that they cook.

Other cookbooks may offer a broad range of cooking styles for the most popular fishes from throughout the region or world. This book consists of recipes tightly tailored for only the seafood found in northern Gulf of Mexico waters. Furthermore, it is complete to those types of seafood commonly considered edible and found in those waters. There are plenty more types of fish and sea creatures inhabiting the northern Gulf of Mexico than those discussed here, but none that most people eat. This compilation is purely designed to examine what people eat and how they eat it in this specific area

The fact is that seafood is easy—maybe the easiest to prepare of all "meat."

The mystery for most is that seafood looks different than a cut of beef or pork or a chicken leg, and that causes some to shy away from cooking seafood. That is a shame. Seafood cooks quickly, can be eyeballed to determine when it is done, and accepts a world of spices and accompaniments to please almost any palate, no matter how coarse or refined. For the purist, it can be politely sautéed, baked, or broiled with salt, pepper, and a pat of butter for the simplest and tastiest of meals.

Preparation of shellfish is a bit more varied than that of finfish because of different flesh textures, edible parts, and cooking times. This book has sections devoted to each type of seafood found in the northern gulf, including preparation details. The bottom line is to not overcook the flesh. If in doubt, sometimes the most basic cooking method is the easiest—and the most enjoyable.

Fish recipes typically divide into two overarching categories: those for lean fish and those for fatty fish. Once you determine whether your fish is a lean or fatty species, you can interchange most of the recipes in this book (although, as previously mentioned, the recipes were designed with a specific fish in mind). Of course, the type of fish that you plan to prepare must be big enough to support the recipe that you plan to use. For example, steaks require a more rounded fish such as tuna, amberjack, king mackerel and some groupers. Fillets are available from almost any species except the smaller panfish such as silver seatrout.

The trick with fish and other seafood is the same for any other meat: simply don't overcook it. Dry seafood isn't good, no matter how you serve it. The flesh lacks connective tissue, so it is guaranteed to be tender. When it flakes with a fork, it is ready to be eaten. After that, match whatever vegetables and spices that you enjoy with the fish you are about to cook, and you will have a memorable meal.

As my Aunt Edith says, "Cook a whole bunch of good stuff together and you'll have something good to eat." That may not always be accurate with some meats, but more often than not, it works with seafood.

As for me, I am not a chef. I am a fish catcher and butcher and a lover of seafood, particularly seafood from the northern Gulf of Mexico, where I have worked and played and fished for a number of years.

My wife, on the other hand, is a great cook who has tailored some of the recipes in this book to make them better than where they started out. Although she does not like for me to do the cooking, I do it a lot anyway. For me, a simple sautéed red snapper fillet requires ten utensils, four pans and a half roll of paper towels—and, of course, the kitchen is a mess when I'm finished. No matter who does the cooking, however, seafood is often center stage.

Celeste Ward, the talented photographer whose beautiful images of plated dishes grace this book, is also an accomplished cook. She writes a food blog for a prominent Alabama news Web site, and she and her cooking skills have been featured on several television programs. In addition to her photographs, she has contributed several delicious recipes to this book.

Besides myself, my wife, and Celeste, most of the dishes here either have come from or have been tailored from recipes developed by a number of local, regional, and national organizations dedicated to the preservation and proper use of America's seafood and marine resources.

Enjoy these recipes—and don't worry if you find yourself in unfamiliar territory. Cooking should take you on a journey, in this case, a journey across the northern gulf coast. There is good food to be eaten.

In addition, I hope that you will engage in and enjoy the whole seafood experience. Buy or borrow a long-handled net or circular crab net and go crabbing. Catch whiting and pompano in the surf and fry it for supper. Learn to throw a circular cast net for mullet (no bait is required, and the nets are inexpensive). Buy a ticket for a party-boat fishing trip, or, if cost is no object, charter a boat and troll for bottom fish. Most importantly, spend time with your family or friends. Capturing most species of fish and shellfish has the potential to be a wonderfully fun family experience. Even if you don't catch or capture anything, exploring a shoreline—bay or surf—will be a fine adventure.

Be brave and clean your own catch if you have the time and aren't too tired. The worst you can do is create some funnily shaped cuts of fish and maybe suffer a finger nick if you are careless. Don't worry that you won't be as slick or as quick as the guys at the fish house. Just have fun! And, the more you practice, the more proficient you will become.

Finally and perhaps most importantly, if you catch fish or shellfish, cook what you catch and let everyone in on it. Pick and boil crabs. Shuck your own oysters and slurp them raw, right from the shell (though not everyone will like the idea of swallowing raw or live shellfish, so don't force this on anyone). Peel and devein your own shrimp. These are all things that everyone in the family can do. Dive in! It never hurts to learn new things, and you will find easy-to-use tips on how to do these things in the following pages.

The only bad thing that can happen is that you take things too seriously and expect nothing less than perfection. Mess-ups can be fun. Laugh at them and set the tone for the rest of your company. In the end, you're still going to have some great seafood to eat and some great memories to look back on. At the end of this journey, you will have had a wonderful time with your family and provided everyone, young and old, with a happy day on the coast while learning something new. What could be wrong with that?

RED SNAPPER
$20.99

USA/WILD

TRIGGER FISH
$18.99
LB.

USA/WILD   EAST COAST

FLOUNDER
$15.99
LB.

USA/WILD

TILAPIA
.99
B.

Acknowledgments

Someone is going to get left out of this, so let me apologize for that right up front. Chalk it up to my being old and forgetful. A lot of folks helped with this book, including some who may not even have realized it when they did what they did:

My wife, Jan, such a good cook that she ought to be running a restaurant (but she won't, because it would cost her face time with her grandchildren). She provided several recipes and tailored others.

Photographer and food blogger Celeste Ward. Rest assured that this will not be the last time you hear of her. Her terrific husband also pitched in. Celeste also had this to say: "I want to thank my wonderful husband, Brad, for his countless hours and late nights in the studio helping to beautifully light and edit the photos found in this book. His passion for photography continues to be a huge inspiration to me, and I could not have done it without his expert assistance."

Paul Balthrop of the Bureau of Seafood and Aquaculture for the Florida Department of Agriculture and Consumer Services; Judy Jamison, executive director of the Gulf and South Atlantic Fisheries Foundation, Inc.; Linda Teuton of the Virginia Marine Products Board; and Christine Patrick of NOAA Fisheries. All of these men and women were so helpful in guiding me to great recipes and in securing permission for them to appear in this book.

Dr. Bob Shipp, chair of the Department of Marine Sciences at the University of South Alabama, who enjoys catching, cooking, and eating seafood almost as much as he does studying it. His expertise on each species of fish and shellfish in the gulf is phenomenal.

Capts. Mike and Skip Thierry, father and son, who run charter boats out of Dauphin Island, Alabama. They know more about finding fish than just about anyone else I know.

Jason Schroeder, manager, and his crew at Sexton's Seafood in the Birmingham, Alabama, suburb of Cahaba Heights. Their generous time and permission to photograph fish market forms and fresh market scenes are a great contribution.

In addition, I would like to thank a host of marine science students, instructors, professors, and marine biologists at the University of South Alabama and the Dauphin Island Sea Lab, who continue to give so many long hours on both sea and land to better understand and to help preserve our marine resources.

Certain organizations are dedicated to the preservation, proper use, and preparation of our seafood resources. While fishermen, conservationists, and government agencies charged with managing our natural resources push and pull at each other without achieving equilibrium, they all have a common goal and play critical roles in the proper, responsible harvesting of our seafood, maintaining a quality environment for the fish and shellfish, and providing food preparation methods that are practical, wholesome, and incredibly tasty. They include the NOAA Fisheries in Washington, DC, the Bureau of Seafood and Aquaculture for the Florida Department of Agriculture and Consumer Services, the Gulf and South Atlantic Fisheries Foundation, and the Virginia Marine Products Board.

More than any other, the Bureau of Seafood and Aquaculture in Florida and the Gulf and South Atlantic Fisheries Development Foundation were of the utmost importance. Their development of recipes for gulf fish provided important guidance on breadth of various types of preparation—from soups to casseroles to grilling, frying, poaching, broiling, and boiling. Plus, their archives of high-quality recipes were important in several ways. In some instances, their recipes are used in this book as presented. In other instances the recipes were used for species other than those that they were specifically manufactured for (with great care being taken to make sure that they could be substituted without loss of flavor). Lastly, many of their recipes were used as a basis for tailoring recipes of the same style. The bureau provided the foundation for dishes involving amberjack, bluefish, croaker, dolphin, drum, flounder, grouper, mullet, pompano, rock shrimp, scallops, sheepshead, snapper, tilefish, triggerfish, tripletail, trout, tuna, and whiting.

The Gulf and South Atlantic Fisheries Foundation represents the gulf seafood industry in the states of Alabama, Florida, Georgia, Louisiana, Mississippi, North Carolina, South Carolina, Texas and Virginia. Their archives contributed to recipes featuring amberjack, bass, crab, croaker, dolphin, drum, flounder, grouper, lobster, mackerel, mullet, oysters, rock shrimp, scallops, shark, sheepshead, shrimp, snapper, squid, tilefish, triggerfish, and trout.

Folks at the Virginia Marine Products Board, although not located on the gulf, developed some terrific recipes with certain species found in our waters, including bluefish, catfish, croaker, flounder, grouper, shark, snapper, and trout.

In addition, the National Oceanic and Atmospheric Administration Fisheries department inspired flavorful catfish, grouper, mackerel, shark, swordfish, tilefish, triggerfish, tripletail, trout, and tuna recipes.

The organizations credited above contributed immensely to the development of all recipes in this book. I would be remiss in not crediting them fully, for their recipes were the inspiration for those included in this volume. What you hold in your hands would not exist without their expertise, passion, and commitment to northern gulf seafood of all shapes and sizes.

Introduction:
What's in the Gulf of Mexico?

There are more than one hundred species of edible fish, plus a couple dozen types of shellfish and crustaceans, living in the Gulf of Mexico. These can be grouped into about thirty different types of finfish and a dozen or so shellfish and crustaceans. For example, there are red, gag, scamp, and several other groupers, but they all cook the same. There are three or four different amberjack species and more than a dozen sharks. The several white snappers (porgies) look so much alike that it takes a marine biologist to tell the difference.

Some fish can be caught or purchased fresh in local markets year around. Grouper, snapper, triggerfish, flounder, and white snapper live in northern gulf waters all of the time. Other fish visit only when the weather suits them. The mackerels come in spring: Spanish arrive first, in March or early April, followed by the larger king mackerel in April or even early May. Cobia begin showing up in March, migrate into northern gulf waters from east to west through the spring, and settle on offshore reefs for the summer. Dolphin (mahi-mahi) show up when the weather warms and disappear when it cools. As a result, you will find them most often in markets during the warm months. Furthermore, some sea creatures are subject to regulated seasons. Bay scallops can be gathered beginning in mid- to late summer. Red snapper season is set by a regulatory agency and seems to change every year. There are also distinct seasons for shrimp, redfish, trout, certain groupers, amberjack, and stone crab, to mention a few others.

If you are set on catching your meal, and you are dead set on a certain species of fish, check with the boat captain before securing your charter or with a local tackle-shop operator. He or she should be able to tell you whether the species you are seeking is available to catch.

Looking at the fish by their lifestyles, they can be divided into three groups: reef fish, pelagic fish, and bay fish.

Much of the northern gulf floor consists of narrow ribbons of natural reef or rock, interspersed with wide expanses of sand or mud bottom. In addition, concrete and metal debris (including ships) have been placed on the floor as artificial reefs. They are tiny spots in a huge expanse of underwater desert. Each reef or wreck is an oasis for marine life, and fish gather at them like camel caravans at watering holes in the Sahara. The fish that gather around the reefs—snapper, grouper, triggerfish, and some jacks—tend to be there year around.

The pelagic fish—mackerel, cobia, some tunas, and dolphin—follow the rising water temperature and baitfish northward. Some hold course along the sandbars. Others tend to keep to deeper water. They all seek baitfish, and, by summer, they tend to congregate around the reefs and wrecks where the baitfish are.

The bay holds spotted seatrout, small grouper, and some drum (both red and black) year around.

Other fish come and go, and when you think you have figured out their patterns, they will show up just where they aren't expected to be. These include flounder, sheepshead, black sea bass, bluefish, redfish, several types of trout, and mullet.

No matter the season, there is always something good to be found in northern gulf waters.

Northern Gulf Style

Crossing Pensacola Bay from Gulf Breeze, Florida, on US 98, there is a spot where five flags fly, each representing a nation that, at some point in history, ruled the city of Pensacola: Spain, France, England, Confederate States, United States. It is a good example of the cultural influences from which the seafood tastes of the northern gulf have evolved.

The French and Spanish brought their cooking styles to Texas, Louisiana, Mississippi, and, to a lesser extent, the Alabama coast. French Canadians blended savory spices with inexpensive, native foods to create what is now known as Cajun cooking. While Spanish and French influence can be found from Mobile Bay all the way across the Florida Panhandle, other influences also shaped seafood preparation.

Certain factors determined the growth of seafood culture, including the kind of seafood available for harvest and the tough life on an isolated frontier. Some port towns such as Destin, Florida, were settled by New England fishermen, who brought their simple cooking style that tended to minimize spices and sauces to allow the natural seafood flavors to prevail.

In the years after the Civil War, this coastal region fell into economic depression. Entertaining was modest. Menus and dining styles were simplified. In 1878, with Federal troops still occupying Mobile, Alabama, the ladies of St. Francis Street Methodist Episcopal Church compiled a cookbook. The directions for the dish *Jam Bolaya* illustrate both the region's poverty and ingenuity with native foods: "Have the lard hot, put in flour, cook to a light brown, with a medium-sized onion. Take the giblets, neck, small part of the wings and feet of your chicken, and put in the lard; add half a tea-cup of prepared tomatoes, two dozen oysters, with their liquor, pepper and salt to taste . . ." It is a meal that would cost pennies, even if the oysters had to be purchased instead of gathered from the bay.

The hearty souls living along the coastline ate fresh seafood when they could get it, but a lack of refrigeration prevented the development of seafood as a significant industry. *The Gulf City Cook Book* ladies offered but a handful of seafood recipes, and only for snapper, redfish, sheepshead, oysters, and shrimp. All were basic.

In 1870, the census listed only 2 commercial fishermen in Alabama, but in the next ten years, there was a dramatic change. By 1880, there were 635 commercial fishermen.

In that decade, commercial refrigeration came to the coast, fisheries flourished, seafood became an important table fare, and the chefs of a growing restaurant trade began tinkering with those basic recipes. Today, they are still tinkering.

Twenty-five years ago, hardly anyone fished for amberjack, and it could not be found on a restaurant menu. Today, few menus are without amberjack. Prior to the 1980s, a zillion triggerfish were killed and thrown back by fishermen who were angry that they stole the bait before a red snapper could get to it. Today grilled, fried, baked, sautéed, or broiled triggerfish is regularly on the chalkboard of the region's toniest restaurants. Thanks to the creative and adventurous chefs of the northern gulf, new recipes, even for species once considered inedible, find their way onto coastal restaurant menus and, over time, become classics.

Across the gulf coast, fishermen and chefs alike have developed unique takes on technique and flavor representative of their cultural and geographic influences. Without their innovation, gulf cuisine would be considerably different from what we know and love today.

The Complete Guide to

NORTHERN GULF SEAFOOD

There are hundreds of types of seafood on the market today. Once you know what you want to eat, how much should you buy? The amount of fish or shellfish needed depends on the type of preparation and, obviously, how hungry you and your dinner companions are.

The following chart is a good guide. Consider smaller portions for appetizers or for use in a casserole or salad.

Type of Seafood	Amount per Serving
Fish, whole	¾ pound
Fish, dressed or pan-dressed	½ pound
Fish, fillets or steaks	⅓ to ½ pound
Fish, sticks	4 to 5 sticks
Clams, in the shell	6 to 8 clams
Crab, cooked meat	¼ to ⅓ pound
Lobster, live	1 small to medium whole lobster
Lobster, cooked meat	¼ to ⅓ pound
Oysters, in the shell	½ dozen
Oysters, shucked	½ pint
Scallops	¼ to ⅓ pound
Shrimp, headless	⅓ to ½ pound
Shrimp, peeled and deveined	¼ to ⅓ pound
Shrimp, cooked meat	¼ to ⅓ pound

Fresh Fish

Fish are categorized many ways, but all of them are lumped into the broad categories of lean or fatty.

Fatty fish have an oil content of greater than 5 percent of its flesh. Since the oil is distributed throughout the flesh of the fish, the flesh tends to be darker than that of leaner fish. The exact percentage of oil in fish flesh depends on such variables as species, season, and even habitat's water depth. Fatty fish do not freeze as well as lean fish and should be thawed and eaten within three months of purchase. Fatty fish include amberjack, bluefish, croaker, mullet, pompano, Spanish and king mackerel, and swordfish.

Lean fish are those with a fat content ranging from .5 percent to no more than 5 percent, with the oil in these fish characteristically concentrated in the liver. These fish maintain quality while frozen for up to six months. The very leanest can be held in the freezer up to a year. Lean fish include black sea bass, black drum, flounder, grouper, shark, sheepshead, almost all snappers, tilefish, triggerfish, and whiting.

When deciding what kind of fish to use, keep in mind that, generally, fish containing higher percentages of oil have more flavor. Lean fish may be substituted for fatty fish in a recipe, but the flavor of the dish may be masked and more frequent basting may be required due to the lower oil content. Also, If a recipe requires frequent handling of a fish, as in chowders, soups, or pickling, a firm-fleshed fish (such as grouper, red snapper, and triggerfish) will retain its shape and have a more pleasing finished appearance.

When selecting a whole fish (just as it comes from the water), or drawn fish (internal organs removed), look for these signs of freshness:
- Bright, clear, and bulging eyes.
- Bright red gills, free of slime. Don't be shy! Lift up the gill cover—called the operculum—right in back of the fish's head and peek underneath.
- Firm and elastic flesh, not brown or dry.
- Characteristically marked and colored skin. If it looks

faded, the quality of the flesh probably is fading fast, too.
- Fresh and mild odor, with no disagreeable, fishy smell. The key term here is *disagreeable*. Fish are fish and all have a distinctive fish odor. If in doubt about what your nose tells you, visit several fish markets or ask friends and acquaintances for recommendations. You will notice a difference between one that deals in fresh fish and one that lets the fish hang around too long. A foul-smelling market will make you swear off fish forever—don't let that happen. Find a good, fresh market, and you will be assured of excellent seafood.

THE COMPLETE GUIDE TO NORTHERN GULF SEAFOOD

Frozen Fish

A high-quality frozen fish will have these characteristics:
- Solidly frozen, not discolored flesh. Check for freezer burn on the flesh (a white, dry appearance around the edges). Examine the package for ice crystals. Those crystals may indicate moisture loss from the flesh that could have resulted from thawing and refreezing.
- Little or no odor.
- Tight packaging. Fish should be wrapped in moisture-proof materials with little, if any, air space between the fish and the wrapping. The quality of the fish wrapped in plastic is generally higher if the plastic is vacuum-sealed.

Shrimp

A fresh shrimp should have the following qualities:
- Firm and translucent flesh, free of black spots. If you are purchasing head-on shrimp, the head should be firmly attached to the tail section. If the front half of the shrimp (the part that contains the entrails) looks mushy, dried,

or discolored, or is barely hanging by a thread to the tail section, that shrimp has been too long in the case.
- Fresh and mild odor.

Cooked shrimp should be pink and have a fresh and mild odor.

Oysters

When these animals are purchased in the shell, they should be alive. You can tell by shells that are closed tightly or will close tightly when tapped. Gaping shells indicate that the shellfish is dead and not edible.

Shucked oysters should have a plump and creamy flesh. The liquor (juice inside the shell) should be clear and the odor fresh and mild.

Crabs and Lobsters

These creatures may be purchased alive and, if so, should show movement and have no disagreeable odor.

Frozen lobsters are sometimes available. The gulf lobster lacks the claws of its New England cousin and is more often sold frozen or iced in markets than the New England lobster.

Crab meat should have a mild odor and appear clean and moist.

Scallops

Scallops should have a sweet odor and, when bought in packages, should not include excess liquid.

The gulf offers the smaller bay scallop, which can be found in markets and can be gathered recreationally in a few locations. The large sea scallop, sometimes found in markets, almost assuredly came from somewhere else.

In General . . .
- Plan to use fresh fish or seafood within two days of purchase. If you cannot use fish within two days, cook or freeze it. Cooked fish maintains quality in the refrigerator at 32 to 40 degrees for two to three days.
- Fresh fish or seafood keep best when loosely wrapped and packed in finely crushed ice to prevent moisture loss. If you are buying seafood at a market, make it the last purchase on your shopping trip. Take it home immediately and put it in the refrigerator or freezer.

THE COMPLETE GUIDE TO NORTHERN GULF SEAFOOD

Fish in the refrigerator are like visiting relatives. The longer they hang around, the less pleasant they are. Buy a fish or catch a fish—either way, get it on ice and/or into the refrigerator as swiftly as possible. Cook it by the second day or freeze it.

How to Handle . . .

Fresh fish. Place fresh fish in the refrigerator in a leak-proof wrapper as soon as possible after purchasing. Store at 35 degrees. If you don't know the temperature of your refrigerator, place the fish in the coldest area.

Frozen fish. Commercially packaged frozen fish should be dated and placed in the freezer immediately after buying. Don't linger at the pastry counter and let the seafood partially thaw; get home with it as quickly as possible and make it the first item you move from the grocery bag to the freezer. Store at 0 degrees or lower to avoid loss of color, flavor, and texture. Limit storage time to retain the true flavor of the fish. Typically, the leaner the fish, the longer it can remain frozen and still have quality flavor and texture when thawed and cooked. Always use seafood that has been in the freezer the longest first.

Fresh shellfish. Shellfish, such as live oysters, lobsters, and crabs, should be kept in a moist, cool place. Shucked oysters and scallops will stay fresh for seven to ten days; shrimp, two to three days; and cooked crab, four to five days, if packed in ice in the refrigerator.

Frozen shellfish. Frozen shellfish should be dated on the packaging and placed in the freezer at 0 degrees or lower immediately after purchase. Most shellfish are commercially frozen to maintain quality for up to one year.

Cooked seafood. Store cooked seafood in the refrigerator or freezer. In the refrigerator, place in a covered container and use within three to four days. For the freezer, pack in a moisture- and vapor-proof container. Cooked seafood can be held for up to three months.

How to Freeze . . .

Seafood may be served throughout the year by freezing good-quality products during peak seasons.

Rapid freezing is important. A rapid freeze creates many small crystals so that the tissue cells are not ruptured. Rapid freezing also reduces the amount of time that bacteria and enzymes have to act on the flesh. Large, bulky packages or inadequate air circulation created by improper spacing in the freezer can prolong the time it takes to thoroughly freeze the fish. The freezer should be turned to its coldest setting prior to freezing and returned to its normal setting once the fish is frozen.

Fish. Before freezing fish, butcher it the way you plan to eat it and in a quantity suitable for one meal. Protect the fish from oxidation (rancidity) and dehydration (freezer burn) by glazing the fish. To glaze, place the fish on a tray, cover with aluminum foil, and freeze. Remove from the foil. Dip frozen fish in ice water to form a glaze. Return to freezer. Repeat process two or three times until the fish is completely glazed. Package fish in cling wrap, aluminum foil, or freezer paper, eliminating air pockets.

Another way to freeze dressed fish, fillets, and steaks is in a sealable plastic bag from which all the air has been removed. Load the bag with cold water. Hold the fish in the closed end and bring the bag out of the water, fish end first. Pulling the bag out upside down like this creates a vacuum, thus eliminating all air. Seal the bag and put it in the freezer.

Fish also may be frozen in block form in waxed cartons (thoroughly cleaned milk cartons, for example), plastic containers, or pans.

Shrimp. Shrimp can be frozen cooked or raw, with the shell on or off. Maximum storage life and quality usually can be obtained by freezing what are commonly called "green headless" shrimp, raw, shell-on tails. The shell offers extra protection against oxidation and dehydration. Shell-on shrimp should be frozen in waxed cartons, plastic containers, or heavy plastic bags that will resist being punctured by the shells.

After a thorough washing, the shrimp should be placed in the container and frozen. After freezing (four to eight hours, depending on the package size and temperature), the plastic containers or waxed cartons should be filled with cold water and refrozen. This will expel the air and create a protective coating on the shrimp.

Blue crabs. Picked blue crab meat does not freeze satisfactorily because of texture and flavor changes that happen during the freezing process. Research indicates that rapidly frozen crab cores (what remains after debacking and cleaning) can be stored without significant quality loss. The thawed cores can be picked prior to consumption.

Crab cores can be prepared in two ways. The live crab can be boiled for twelve to fifteen minutes, debacked, gills and entrails removed, then washed and frozen. The other method requires debacking, cleaning, washing, then boiling and freezing. The second method probably is better, since less handling is involved after the crab is cooked. Rapid cooling after cooking is essential, so individual cores should be wrapped and frozen or frozen and glazed as rapidly as possible before they are wrapped in a larger package.

Oysters, clams, and scallops. People often are disappointed when they expect frozen oysters, clams, and scallops to taste as good as fresh ones. It is almost impossible to avoid changes in flavor, texture, and color during frozen storage. With proper handling and freezing techniques, these changes are not severe, especially if the product is cooked immediately after thawing.

Shell oysters and clams should be alive at the time of purchase and can be kept alive for seven to ten days if stored in a moist, cool place. Do not shuck oysters or clams that will not close after being tapped lightly on the shell. Wash the outside of the shell before shucking. Shuck oysters and clams into a strainer (the liquor should be clear and can be saved) and wash the oyster and clam meat to remove sand and pieces of shell. Place shellfish in a container and cover with water. Use small containers to ensure rapid freezing. Scallops are shucked and packed in ice at sea. They are available fresh or frozen.

Lobster. Whole lobster or lobster tails, raw or cooked, may be frozen. Since the shell protects them from drying out, glazing is not necessary but recommended, particularly if the lobster is to be kept for longer than four months. The exposed meat on lobster tails should be protected by tight wrapping. Cover the lobsters in freezer paper and place in the freezer set to 0 degrees Fahrenheit or lower.

How to Thaw . . .

Schedule thawing of fish and shellfish so it can be cooked soon after it is thawed. Do not store thawed seafood for more than one day before cooking. One effective way to thaw seafood products is under cold running water. Allow a half hour per pound with this method. Seafood also may be thawed in the refrigerator. A one-pound package thaws in eighteen to twenty-four hours. The lowest cycle on a microwave oven may be used for thawing seafood products. To retain quality, seafood should be thawed quickly, but never at room temperature or in warm water. Do not refreeze. Frozen seafood may be cooked without thawing, if additional cooking time is allowed. However, if the fish is going to be prepared stuffed, breaded, or cooked with a sauce, thawing is recommended.

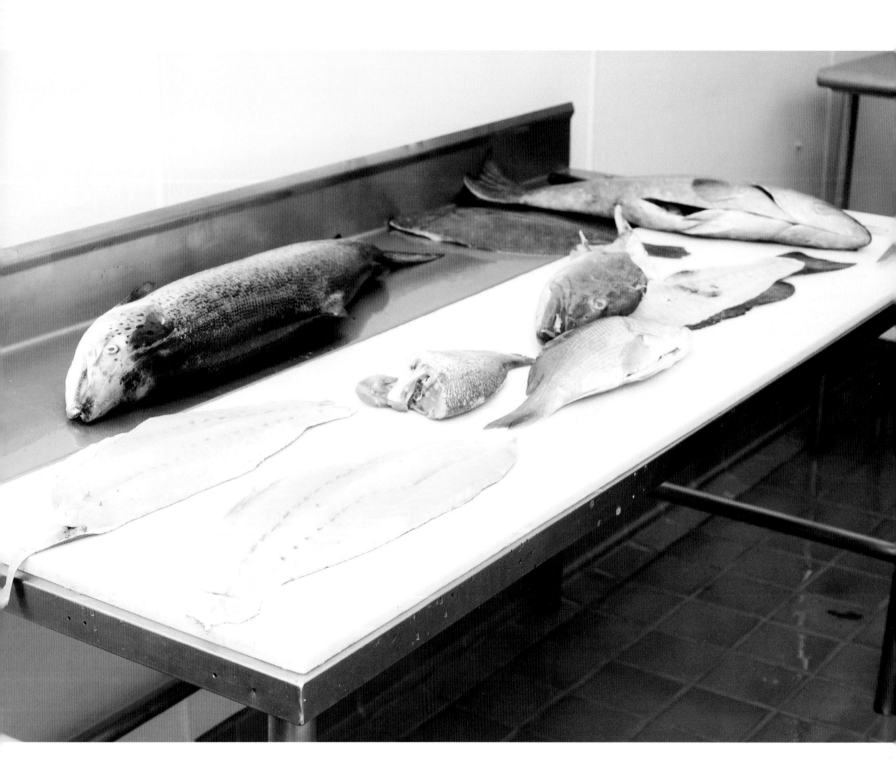

Most experts will tell you that there are six basic market forms of fish: whole or round, drawn, dressed or pan-dressed, steaks, fillets, and butterfly fillets. However, I have friends who insist on using dull knives and inventing new cuts of fish every time they are lucky enough to visit a fish-cleaning station—they hack and whack and usually require a trip to the drugstore for adhesive bandages after every fish-cleaning adventure. I have wondered whether the consumption of cold beverages, which often takes place around fish-cleaning stations, could have anything to do with the creativity and carelessness that takes place. My friends seem to always have huge amounts of fun at the cleaning station, so don't discount their efforts. What's left when they finish is still a nice batch of tasty fish, even if the cuts look a little—or maybe a lot—weird.

Don't be discouraged by my friends' recklessness. The basic cuts, or market forms, of fish, are not difficult to master. Following are cuts that they should have had when the task was complete:

Whole or round. The fish just as it comes from the water. Before cooking, the fish must be scaled and gutted to remove its internal organs. Usually, the person cleaning the fish also removes the head and fins before cooking. The fish can then be cooked as is, filleted, or cut into steaks or cubes.

Drawn. The whole fish, entrails removed. To prepare for cooking, follow the procedure for whole or round fish.

Dressed or pan-dressed. The whole fish with the scales, entrails, and usually the head and fins removed. The fish may then be cooked, filleted, or cut into steaks or cubes.

Fillets. The lengthwise cuts of fish, typically boneless or near-boneless. Small fish bones sometimes hide in fillets only to reveal themselves after being cooked, so be careful. Fillets are ready to cook as purchased.

Steaks. The cross-section cuts of large, dressed fish. They are ready to cook as purchased.

Butterfly fillets. Two single fillets held together by a small portion of skin or flesh. Actually, it is a curiosity why this is considered a basic cut of fish. Also, it is hard to understand why anyone would go to the trouble of preparing a cut of fish in this manner when two separate fillets would work just as well with almost all recipes.

Cleaning and Dressing Fish

If you catch fish while fishing on your own, you typically are stuck cleaning the fish. If you catch fish while on a party boat or charter boat, or if you purchase fish fresh from the market, you have a few options. Those options have plusses and minuses.

If you are a decent fish butcher, you will get more yield when you clean the fish yourself. This is because you will (most likely) take more time getting that last little nugget of flesh and will be (most likely) more careful when filleting to keep the knife blade near the bone. Waste not, want not.

On the other hand, after a hot, long day on the water when you find yourself standing, covered with dried salt spray and fish slime, cleaning your catch may not be the thing that you want to do most. At that moment, a hot shower followed by a cold beverage probably will be among your first priorities. If this is the case, pay a fish butcher, console yourself that you may not get as much flesh as had done the job yourself, and go clean up.

Fish cleaning comes with the cost of a charter for many boats. The butcher usually is the deck hand. By the end of the day, he or she wants to get home and clean up as much as you do, so even though there are few fish butchers better than a good deck hand, he or she isn't going to take pains to reap every last morsel. Also, if the deck hand has worked hard all day, as most do, it would be nice to pay him or her a little extra for the fish cleaning.

At some docks, a central fish-cleaning operation handles the butchering chore rather than the deck hands. The result is about the same. These guys are experts. It is amazing how swiftly they can butcher a fish. However, they have to move fast in order to stay even with the flow of fish arriving at the door, so they too may not be as careful in getting every last bit of meat. These operations usually charge by the pound of uncleaned fish.

Workers at most fresh markets will butcher a fish in almost any manner that you wish. Typically, the butchering does not cost extra, or, if it does, very little. Unless they are swamped, market butchers will take more time to provide you with maximum yield and will provide whatever cuts you desire. When they are through, they will package everything—including the carcass—if you want them to.

If you decide to clean your fish yourself, you will need a sharp knife, a cutting board, and fresh running water. Some notes:

The knife. The edge is a lot more important than the blade. I've seen people use inexpensive, four-inch Rapala knives and what looked to have been the curved blade of a scimitar. Something in between probably is best—a six-inch, thin, sharp blade, and maybe a second knife with a strong, serrated edge to whack through rib bones. Cheap knives are just as good as expensive ones, so long as they will hold a sharp edge. Find something with which you are comfortable. Some tackle shops will sell used knives from commercial fish houses at bargain prices; in most cases, the blade has been sharpened so many times that it is way narrower than it was originally. For the casual fish cleaner, however, it still has years of life left. Plus, as one friend said, it already knows what to do. There is one knife preferred by the more fumble-fingered of fish cleaners: one that floats. Many fish-cleaning stations are over water at the end of a dock. There is some attraction about a nice bone-handled or solid-handled knife that draws it to the water. Few are the fish cleaners who want to jump in to retrieve the blade, no matter how beloved it might be. Some argue that a wood- or hollow-handled knife never falls into the water, but that is not true. It is true, however, that you remain a lot drier by retrieving a floating knife than diving for a sinking one.

The cutting board. A number of fish-cleaning stations are made of metal, probably for reasons of sanitation and odor. On a sunny summer day, it gets so hot that a fish could almost fry right there on the cutting surface. If you are one of the creative fish cleaners such as those mentioned above, a metal cutting surface does wonders at dulling a sharp blade. Find something to sit on the metal. Most kitchen shop cutting boards are made of great material—wood, bamboo, or some sort of manufactured stuff that is hard enough to hold up under pressure and soft enough not to torment a sharp blade. The trouble is that most kitchen boards are made for trimming a pork chop, not cleaning a fifteen-pound red snapper. If you want a store-bought item, it needs to be a whopper, maybe a couple of feet long. Keep in mind that keeper amberjack and cobia must exceed two feet in length. A better option is to use a board two inches high, twelve inches wide, and about two and a half feet long. Treated and finished lumber is not needed—we are not building a deck here, after all. Put the board on top of the metal, wash it down, clean the fish, and wash it down again. Now you know why you see chunks of lumber laying around fish-cleaning stations for no apparent reason.

Running water. Fish are slick and slimy. The slime is a protective coating when they are alive. Wash it off so that you can get a good grip on your fish when cleaning it and so that the slime doesn't smear all over the flesh. When you are finished cleaning each fish, wash away the scales, guts, slime, and other scraps so that you have a clean starting place for the next fish. When you are done, give everything a good scrubbing and wash it down. No one wants to come behind you and find a grimy, smelly cleaning station.

Following are step-by-step directions for preparing the basic market forms of fish:

Dressed

1. Lay the whole fish on a board and hold firmly. Using a scaler, dull knife, or large tablespoon, scrape from tail to head to remove scales.

2. Cut entire length of belly. Remove entrails and pelvic fin.

3. Using a sharp knife, remove head and pectoral fins by cutting in front of the collarbone.

4. Remove the dorsal fin by cutting along the length of each edge. Grasp trailing edge of fin between the thumb and flat of knife blade and give a quick pull toward the head. Clean and rinse fish thoroughly.

Steaks (Large Fish Only)

1. Follow steps 1 through 4 for dressed fish.

2. Cut fish across backbone into pieces approximately ¾-inch thick.

1. Follow step 1 of dressed fish, unless the fish is to be skinned.

2. Cut along back of fish from tail to head.

If fish is to be skinned:

1. Cut down to backbone just behind pectoral fin. Turn knife flat and slide along backbone to tail. Turn fish over and repeat process.

2. To skin, place fillet skin side down on a board. Hold tail section firmly. As close to tail as possible, insert knife between skin and flesh. Hold knife blade flat (parallel to board) and push knife forward while pulling the free end of skin firmly with fingers.

An important note (if you want to keep your knife sharp and your language at the "G" rating): when making cuts into the fish, angle your blade so that it goes between the fish's scales rather than through them. Fish scales attach to the fish on the edge nearest the fish's head. The tail side of each scale is loose. This means that inserting your knife blade at a slight angle toward the head and allowing it to find its way between the scales. Hacking through scales is like scrubbing the edge on a whetstone—it's not good for you or your knife.

Also, when preparing skinless fillets, some find it easier to follow step 1 but leave the fillet attached at the tail by a small amount of skin. This allows the fillet to be flipped like a book page away from the fish so that the skin side rests on the board. By leaving the fillet attached by this small amount of skin, you can use the fish as an anchor to hold for working through step 2. Having the body of the fish to hold on to, particularly when your hands are slippery (which they will be), usually makes the process easier and quicker.

A note about triggerfish: Because these fish have extremely tough and leathery skin, they call for a different cleaning technique. Those skilled with an electric knife sometimes cut through the skin and fillet the fish as mentioned above. However, filleting with a non-electric knife is best done with a few additional steps:

1. Run your index finger along the top of the head from front to back. At the place where the bone ends and the flesh begins, insert the blade of a sharp fillet knife through the skin but not the flesh. With the sharp edge of the knife pointed up, slide the blade from the insertion point to the tail to separate the skin from the flesh.
2. Go back to where you inserted the knife point right behind the head, insert the knife point at the same location and then cut a slit perpendicular to the first cut, basically from the top to the bottom of the fish.
3. Without removing the knife tip, turn the blade 90 degrees and cut a half-inch-long slit along the belly to snap the ribs and break the whole fillet away from the body of the fish.

4. Remove the knife blade, grab an edge of the skin at the top of the fish and pull hard toward the tail. The skin will tear off, leaving the flesh intact. Throw away the skin or, as one fisherman claimed he has done, dry it out and make yourself a pair of shoes.
5. Repeat the process on the other side of the fish.
6. Once the skin is removed, removed the fillets using the previous instructions.

A note about amberjack: These are big fish, and hacking through the large rib bones can quickly dull a knife, if not ruin it. There is a technique that expert fish butchers employ that looks easy but requires some practice. The technique is to fillet the fish, skin on, cutting around the rib cage rather than through it.

1. Cut a small hole near the tail of the fish big enough for a finger.
2. Grasp the amberjack in front of the tail, and hold it up as high as your arm will reach. (This requires some strength, since amberjack are large fish.)
3. Inserting a finger in the hole, pull downward swiftly and with some vigor. The rib bones should snap away like dry twigs.

This may sound easy, but you will look like a fool until you get the hang of it. The technique is a huge time- and knife-saver once you master it.

Some fish cleaners don't care about the meat between and around fish ribs. The ribs are sharp, numerous, and quickly can dull a sharp blade. If you don't want to bother with the extra hassle, here's what to do:

1. Make the cut behind the head as explained above.
2. Slide the blade down the fish's backbone from head to tail, but don't go into the rib cage. Stop your knife point at the spine and work back toward the tail until you have cleared the rib cage.
3. Push the knife blade to the bottom of the fish and continue the fillet process.
4. Go back and cut just above the rib cage from front to back until the fillet releases.

Butterfly Fillets

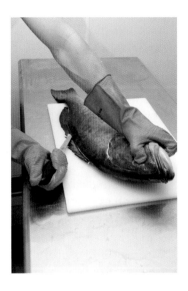

1. Follow steps 1 and 3 for dressed fish.

2. Beginning at the head, cut lengthwise along the backbone to the tail. Don't cut the flesh and skin of the belly. Lay fish open, exposing the body cavity. Remove entrails. Clean and rinse fish thoroughly.

One last tidbit: a little rigor mortis can be a good thing, particularly where fish cleaning is concerned. If you are too quick to the dock, your catch may still be flopping. Not only does it try not to get filleted, for some it also seems less pleasant to butcher a live creature than a dead one, even though the end result is the same. If you have caught fish and thrown them in the cooler but returned to the dock before they stiffened up, the flesh can wobble around and make filleting more difficult. This occurs particularly in larger fish. The easiest fish cleaning is with a fish that has been laid flat in the cooler and that has been in the cooler long enough to get stiff. We're not talking about a fish being dead for days—we're talking about fish that have been thoroughly iced but are only two to eight hours from being caught. A flat, stiff fish butchers more easily because the fish does not flop and the flesh does not wobble while you are working.

Snapper and Grouper Throats

There is a cut of snapper and grouper that coastal fishermen consider the tastiest cut of either fish, but it is found only in select locally owned and operated restaurants and fresh markets. It is the throat. If comments by Andrew Zimmern on his strange-food television show are accurate, then indeed this may be the best part of the fish. On fish of five pounds or larger, the throat can be as large as a chicken breast. Even though it contains several funky-shaped bones, they are large and easily worked around. If you can find throats in the market, you're lucky. If not, you will have to either purchase a fish whole or catch your own.

The throat has the general shape of a full chicken breast, and, like the chicken breast, is often split down the middle. Cut through, it provides two flat pieces of meat. Alternatively, it can be butterflied so that both sides of the throat will lay flat for cooking.

Throats can be prepared in most of the same ways as other grouper, snapper, and large, lean fish. Grilling and frying are probably the two most popular cooking methods for this cut. Whatever spices and seasonings that you enjoy on other seafood dishes will work with throats.

The throat is that part of the fish below the backbone, behind the gills, and back toward the belly. Some say that the throat ends just in front of the pectoral fins. Others, however, include the muscle group that works the pectoral fins. In fact, some throat experts say that they leave on the pectoral fins because they make good "handles" when eating the fish. Says one fisherman, "Just cut as much stuff away that doesn't look like meat, and you'll be fine." However, I feel that more precise directions are in order.

A sharp knife and a pair of small sharp shears are handy to separate the throat from the fish. Also, there is an additional question to answer: to scale or not to scale? Some fishermen advise not to bother scaling the throat if you plan to grill it. After grilling, the meat pulls away from the skin, which is discarded. Others advise to scale the throat while the fish is whole, and that this should be done if the fish it to be prepared by any method other than grilling. After scaling (or not scaling) your fish, fillet it per previous direction. Then:

1. With the knife, cut from lower throat latch (gill slot) angling upward to intersect your filet cut behind the head. Turn the fish over and do the same on the other side.

2. The throat will be held under the fish's chin by a small segment of bone. Snip it with the knife or shears. This will result in a large lump of meat.

3. Rinse to clear any random scales and other residue.

Basic Cooking Techniques

If you learn nothing else from this book, learn this: No matter how you choose to cook seafood, timing is the real secret. Fish is done when the flesh becomes opaque and flakes easily with a fork. Overcooking toughens and dries the flesh.

Here is a simple and practical method of timing fish. Measure the fish fillet or steak at its thickest part. Allow ten minutes of cooking time per inch of thickness. For fish measuring less than one inch, shorten cooking time proportionately. Double the cooking time for fish still frozen. If fish is cooked in foil or in sauce, allow an extra five minutes per inch. Periodically test for doneness to avoid overcooking.

The basic cooking methods fall into eleven categories. Start with whichever you enjoy most, add as few or as many ingredients as you like, and everything will be just fine.

Baking. This is method uses dry heat. To bake, place the fish in a greased baking dish, being sure to keep it moist and flavorful with seasoned oil, sauce, or any condiment of your choice. Fillets and steaks adapt easily to many recipes that require baking. A dressed fish may be stuffed with herb and bread stuffing and baked with the head and tail still attached. However, more genteel cooks don't like their food to stare back at them, so don't be afraid to lop off the head. Bake in a 350-degree oven until the fish flakes easily when tested with a fork. Cooking time varies according to thickness of the fish.

Boiling. Bring water and salt (one quart water for two tablespoons salt) to a rolling boil in a large pot. Add seafood and return to a boil; reduce heat, maintaining a slow boil or, better, a simmer. Shrimp is done in two to four minutes; rock shrimp in thirty-five to forty seconds; lobster and crab in twelve to fifteen minutes, and finfish in eight to ten minutes. Shellfish and fish are boiled when they are to be served with a sauce or flaked and combined with other ingredients. Cooks in the Carolinas and Louisiana have made quite an art of boiled seafood, with one especially popular dish known as the Lowcountry boil. The idea is a basic dish of good things thrown in a pot: crabs, shrimp, pieces of boneless fish, one-inch segments of kielbasa sausage, new potatoes, corn on the cob, and some good seafood seasoning (many enjoy Old Bay and some of the Cajun seasonings, but there are plenty of others). There are lots of versions of this dish. Find one that sounds the tastiest to you and go at it.

Broiling. To cook by direct, intense heat, a pan-dressed fish fillet or steak works best. Place the fish in a single layer on a well-greased broiler pan. The fish should be four to six inches from the source of heat. Cooking time usually is between eight and ten minutes. Turn thicker pieces, such as pan-dressed fish, halfway through the cooking time, and baste. Baste well with oil or basting sauce before and during cooking. Fat fish require less basting than lean fish. Trust your eyes to tell you the amount of basting needed to keep the fish moist.

Deep-fat frying. Any cooking method that involves frying will not be the first choice of the most health conscious among us. Eating too much fried food clogs up our blood vessels and lowers our overall health. But Southerners do love it, and preparing a dish with the three basic Southern food groups—meat, flour and grease—results in a mighty tasty dish. So, if you hope to perpetuate your Southern heritage, here's what to do: fill the fryer no more than half full of oil to allow room for fish and bubbling oil; heat to 350 to 375 degrees. Place breaded or battered fish, one layer at a time, in the fry basket so the pieces do not touch. Fry in deep oil until the fish is brown and flakes easily with a fork. Before frying additional fish, be sure the oil returns to the correct temperature.

Grilling. The pan-dressed, fillet, or steak cuts of fish are best for grilling. Charcoal, electric, or gas grills work equally well. The big trick here is knowing how to flip the fish without breaking the fillet and allowing part of it to fall through the grill. Thick cuts are preferable because they are too big to fall through the grill grate. For those less skilled in turning fish on a grill, the best crutch is a well-greased, long-handled, hinged wire grill. It is a contraption that incarcerates the fish and prevents it from escaping through the grate, making it much easier to turn. It does not diminish the quality of the cooked fish. Baste the fish with sauce before and during grilling. Grill approximately four to six inches from moderately hot briquettes for ten to twenty minutes, depending on the thickness of the fish. Fish is done when it flakes easily with a fork.

Microwave cooking. To cook in a microwave oven, follow your manufacturer's directions for best results. Oven settings can vary from one microwave to the next. Seafood is generally cooked at a high setting, which radiates the most power and cooks food quickly to retain natural goodness, texture, and flavor. Like other cooking methods, when in doubt, trust your eye test to determine most precisely when the fish is done.

Oven frying. This might not carry quite as many calories as the deep-fat and pan-frying methods, but it still uses oil. However, it does allow cooks to pretend that they are preparing a much healthier dish, because it employs the oven. Fish cooked by this method does not require turning

or basting. Because this allows a large amount of fish to be cooked at once, it is a good option if you are feeding a large number of people. Dip fish in salted milk (a milk and egg wash works well too; its main purpose it to give the breading something to hold on to) and coat with any breading mixture that you enjoy. Place fish in a shallow, well-greased baking pan. Pour melted fat or oil over the fish and bake in an extremely hot oven, 500 degrees, until fish flakes easily with a fork. Cooking time will be short.

Pan-frying. This achieves a similar result as deep frying, but the process is different in that you don't sink the fish into a pot of oil. Instead, heat about 1/8 inch of oil in the bottom of a heavy frying pan. Place breaded fish in a single layer in the hot oil. Do not overload the pan. Fry fish at a moderate temperature until lightly browned on one side, then turn over and cook on the other side until browned.

Poaching. Poached fish tends to come off a little bland, so it most often is used as a main dish with a sauce, as a primary ingredient in a casserole, or chilled and flaked for a salad or dip. To poach, place fish in a single layer in a wide, shallow pan. Barely cover with a liquid, which can be lightly salted water, water seasoned with herbs and spices, milk, or a mixture of white wine and water, depending on the flavor profile that you want to achieve. If in doubt, use the one with which you are comfortable. Nothing magic here—it will taste good. Simmer fish for five to eight minutes or until it flakes easily with a fork.

Steaming. This cooking style has become quite popular with restaurants in recent years, with a number of restaurants devoting whole menu sections to steamed seafood. To do it yourself, use a deep pan with a tight cover. If a steam cooker is not available, anything that prevents the fish from touching the water can serve as a steaming rack. The water may be plain or seasoned with various spices. Bring water to a rapid boil. Place fish on a well-greased rack. Cover the pan tightly and steam for eight to ten minutes.

Smoking. This involves a similar process as grilling with a charcoal, electric or gas grill. To smoke, keep the grill closed while cooking, and add aromatic wood chips, often water-soaked, to the coals to give the fish a smoky flavor. Place fish on the grill, skin-side down, and baste frequently during cooking. Cooking time varies with weather, heat of the grill, amount of moisture in chips, type of grill, and distance of fish from the source of heat, so keep a close eye on the fish so that it doesn't overcook.

Crab Cakes

Blue Crab

Blue crab, like other crabs, have five pairs of legs, the first pair being equipped with menacing pincers. Along with the hard shell that sports various sharp edges, crevices, and spikes, it is a marvel of self-protection. Fortunate—and rare—is the crabber who suffers no cuts or nicks after a day of catching, cleaning, and cooking crabs.

Crabbing can be a fun family outing. Inexpensive crab nets are available at most tackle and bait shops and convenience stores. Simply tie something a crab likes to eat in the bottom of the net: chicken necks, fish carcasses, or any other meat with which a crab cannot easily make off. Drop the net off a dock, pier, or sea wall and periodically pull it up to see if crabs are inside. Some crabbers also bring along long-handled dip nets in order to scoop up crabs that they spot while wading in shallow water. Don't keep the little crabs, of which you will see plenty. Let them grow up. When fully grown, a blue crab averages five to seven inches across the shell from tip to tip. In addition, when catching your own crabs, it is customary to throw back the egg-bearing females, easily recognized by the orange mass of eggs protruding from beneath the apron. In some areas, there are laws against harvesting these females.

Blue crabs are caught and marketed in both the hard-shell and soft-shell stages. Soft-shell crabs are available fresh or frozen. Frozen soft-shell blue crabs should be solidly frozen when purchased. Hard-shell crabs are sold either alive or as cooked meat, fresh or pasteurized. Fresh or pasteurized cooked crab meat usually is available as:
- Lump meat—solid lumps of white meat from the back fin of the body.
- Special or flake meat—small pieces of white meat from the body.
- Claw meat—a brownish-tinted meat from the claws.

When using recipes where appearance of the meat is not important, claw meat is a good choice since its taste is equal to the other forms; it simply doesn't look as pretty or cost as much.

Crab claws with the pincer intact make a delicious crab claw hors d'oeuvre. Alternatively, the dark meat can be removed and used in soups, casseroles, or salads. Crab claws also can be breaded and deep-fat fried for thirty to forty-five seconds or until golden brown. Additionally, basic stuffing recipes based on crab meat are generally so versatile as to be excellent with many other seafoods, particularly lobster, shrimp, and flounder.

To clean a blue crab:

1. With the cooked crab upside down, grab the legs on one side firmly with one hand. With the other hand, lift the flap (apron) and pull back and down to remove the top shell.

2. Turn the crab right side up, remove the gills, and wash out the intestines and spongy material.

3. With a twisting motion, pull the legs loose from the body and discard. Keep any meat that sticks to the legs. Break off the claws.

4. Slice off the top of the inner skeleton and remove all exposed meat.

5. Toward the back of the crab, on each side, lies a large lump of meat. With a careful U-shaped motion of the knife, remove this back fin meat.

6. Remove the white flake meat from other pockets with the point of the knife.

7. Crack the claw shell and remove the shell and the moveable pincer. This will expose the claw meat.

Blue crabs that have recently molted their exoskeleton but are still soft are called soft-shell crabs. To clean a soft-shell crab:

1. Cut off the front of the crab, where its eyes and mouth are, with a pair of kitchen scissors. The cut should be approximately ½ inch behind the eyes.

2. Squeeze the crab to force out the gunk in the sack right behind the cut.

3. Turn the crab on its back and cut off the apron at the back of the shell.

4. Carefully lift up the soft outer shell and clean out the gills, being sure to leave the shell attached.

5. Rinse the crab, dry, and cook immediately.

When purchasing live crabs, allow three hard-shelled crabs per person. One pound of lump, special, or claw meat is enough to feed six people.

Since freezing cooked crabmeat is unsuccessful, the best way to preserve crab meat for one to two months is to freeze it raw. To do this, remove the claws and the inner pod of cartilage containing the body meat and discard the rest of the crab. Freeze the uncracked claws and unpicked pod of meat in a block of ice.

Stone Crab

These crabs can be found in many of the same areas as blue crabs—among rocks, along jetties, or in burrows on sandy or grassy flats.

Only the claw of the stone crab is eaten. Laws in most states forbid harvesting whole stone crabs or removing crab claws when the length of the forearm is less than 2¾ inches. The body generally does not have enough meat to bother with, and, if you harvest only the claw, the crab eventually will grow another claw that can be re-harvested. Most people opt to purchase commercially harvested claws from seafood markets.

Since freezing or icing raw stone crab claws causes the meat to stick to the inside of the shell, they should be cooked immediately. Those purchased commercially already are cooked. Cooked stone crab claws, unlike blue crab meat, freeze well in the shell, making it possible to buy cooked stone crab claws refrigerated or frozen. When buying cooked stone crab claws, freshness can only be judged by a mild odor. Stone crab meat is extremely rich. Usually, three large claws are enough to satisfy a person.

Store cooked stone crab claws at 32 to 35 degrees for no longer than two or three days. If purchased freshly cooked and frozen in the shell the same day, the shelf life of the frozen claw is about six months. Always examine cooked claws for broken joints or cracks in the shell before freezing. The shell protects the meat during freezing and eliminates the necessity of block freezing or glazing. Only freeze claws that are intact.

To serve stone crab claws:

1. Crack all sections of the shell with a hammer or nutcracker before serving.

2. Remove the shell and movable pincer, leaving the meat attached to the remaining pincer.

The claw is a good hors d'oeuvre or appetizer. Approximately two and a half pounds cooked stone crab claws yields one pound of meat. Many people prefer stone crab meat cold or steamed only long enough to heat it and served with clarified butter or a warm lemon butter.

The cooked meat can be picked from the shell and used in any recipe that includes cooked crab meat or lobster.

Blue Crab Imperial

2 lbs. crab meat
1 tsp. salt
1 tsp. dry mustard
1 tsp. Worcestershire sauce
½ tsp. white pepper
¾ cup mayonnaise, plus additional for topping

Preheat oven to 375 degrees. Combine crab meat, salt, mustard, Worcestershire sauce, white pepper, and mayonnaise. Fill 8 to 10 crab shells with crab mixture. Lightly top with additional mayonnaise. Bake for 20 minutes or until the top is browned. Serves 6 to 8.

Blue Crab Stuffing

1 lb. blue crab meat, cooked
½ cup chopped onion
⅓ cup chopped celery
⅓ cup chopped green pepper
2 cloves garlic, minced
⅓ cup butter, melted, or cooking oil
2 cups soft bread crumbs
2 eggs, beaten
1 tbsp. chopped parsley
1 tsp. salt
½ tsp. pepper

Remove any pieces of shell or cartilage from crab meat. Cook onion, celery, green pepper, and garlic in butter until tender but not brown. In a large bowl, combine crab, vegetables, bread crumbs, eggs, parsley, salt, and pepper, and mix well. Makes enough stuffing for 6 ¾-lb. fish.

Note: Some cooks like to add a little Worcestershire sauce, about ¼ tsp. or so. It is a nice touch.

Also, this basic stuffing can be augmented to make crab cakes or deviled crab.

Boiled Blue Crab

⅓ cup salt
6 quarts boiling water
24 live hard-shell blue crabs
1 package commercial crab boil, optional

Add salt to boiling water. Place live crabs in the water along with commercial crab boil, if desired. Cover and return to the boiling point. Reduce heat and simmer for 12 to 15 minutes until shells are red. Drain. Rinse in cold water. Serve hot or cold. Serves 6.

Crab Cakes

1 recipe Blue Crab Stuffing
1 tsp. prepared horseradish
1 tsp. Worcestershire sauce
¼ tsp. dry mustard
Mayonnaise, optional
1 cup soft bread crumbs

To the blue crab stuffing, add horseradish, Worcestershire sauce, and dry mustard. If mixture seems dry, add a little mayonnaise. Divide mixture equally to form 6 large or 12 small cakes. Roll cakes in bread crumbs. Place cakes in a heavy fry pan containing ⅛ inch of hot oil. Fry at moderate heat until brown on both sides. Serves 6.

Note: Some cooks like to add a teaspoon of Old Bay Seasoning (good on everything, you know) and/or Dijon mustard (anywhere from a teaspoon to a tablespoon, depending on your taste).

West Indies Salad

1 lb. lump blue crab meat
½ cup salad oil
½ cup ice water
½ cup cider vinegar
1 onion, finely chopped
Salt and pepper to taste

Place crab meat in bowl. Add salad oil, ice water, cider vinegar, onion, salt, and pepper to crab meat; chill in refrigerator several hours before eating. Toss lightly before serving. Serves 4 to 6.

Crab Cakes

Deviled Crab

1 recipe Blue Crab Stuffing
1 10¾-oz. can condensed cream of
    mushroom soup
½ tsp. Worcestershire sauce
½ tsp. dry mustard
¼ tsp. hot sauce

Preheat oven to 375 degrees. To the blue crab stuffing, add cream of mushroom soup, Worcestershire sauce, dry mustard, and hot sauce. Mix well and place mixture in six individual crab shells. Bake for 15 to 20 minutes or until heated through. Serves 6.

Natalie's Crab Dip

1 8-oz. package cream cheese, softened
1 tbsp. Dijon mustard
2 green onions, finely chopped
½ medium red or green bell pepper, finely
    chopped
½ cup shredded Cheddar cheese
1 8-oz. can crab meat, drained
Crackers, for serving

Mix all ingredients in a medium-sized bowl; chill. Serve with crackers of your choice. Makes approximately 1½ cups.

Note: This recipe comes from my daughter-in-law, Natalie. Some cooks add ½ tsp. Worcestershire sauce, 1 tsp. Old Bay seasoning, 1 tsp. mayonnaise, or the juice of a lemon wedge. Natalie doesn't include those items, and this dip always disappears at family gatherings. The additions would be good too, but this combination does not require it.

Southern Soft-Shell Crab Amandine

6 soft-shell blue crabs, cleaned
1 egg, slightly beaten
1 tbsp. plus ½ cup water, divided
6 tbsp. all-purpose flour, divided
6 tbsp. butter, divided
1 cup fresh orange juice
1 tsp. brown sugar
½ cup slivered almonds
½ cup orange sections
3 cups wild rice, cooked according to package
    directions

Wash crabs thoroughly, drain well, and dry. Combine egg and 1 tbsp. water. Dip crabs into egg mixture, then into 4 tbsp. flour. Sauté in 3 tbsp. butter for 3 to 4 minutes until crabs are cooked. Remove from pan onto a warm platter. In a frying pan, add remaining 3 tbsp. butter and 2 tbsp. flour; stir until smooth. Add orange juice, remaining ½ cup water, and brown sugar, stirring constantly over low heat, until sauce is thick and bubbly. Add almonds and orange sections. Serve crabs, topped with sauce, over hot wild rice. Serves 6.

Lobster

Two types of lobster are found along the northern gulf: the spiny lobster and the shovelnose or bulldozer lobster.

The spiny lobster also is known as the Florida lobster, sea crawfish, or crayfish. It is a beautifully colored crustacean mottled with brown, green, and blue and dotted with light yellow or white spots on the tail.

The shovelnose lobster is a more rusty color. While the tail essentially is the same shape as that of the spiny lobster, the head and body are much abbreviated, with the head shaped like a shovel, hence its name.

The two species are interchangeable in recipes that call for lobster. Primarily, meat comes from the tail section, since neither species have the large, meat-filled claws characteristic of the northern lobster. These lobsters can be obtained live at certain times of year and either frozen or fresh throughout the rest of the year. A favorite activity of divers is to gather lobsters on dive trips. In fresh markets, often only the tails are sold. Like other shellfish, if purchased live, the lobster must show movement.

When purchasing lobster, prepare a whole, 1-pound lobster per person. However, when used in combination with other ingredients, 1 pound of cooked lobster meat will serve 6. A whole, 1-pound lobster will yield approximately ⅓ pound of lobster meat.

Cooked lobster can easily be recognized, because the shell turns bright red-orange and the meat is snowy white with tinges of red on the membrane surrounding the meat.

This reddish membrane sometimes becomes tough when a cooked lobster is frozen, and it may need to be removed before serving. Cooked lobster will maintain quality in the refrigerator for 2 to 3 days.

Lobster must be handled with care to preserve quality after purchase. Freeze lobster live for best quality. The shell protects the meat from drying out, so no glazing or block freezing is needed unless the lobster is kept for more than four months. Frozen, cooked lobster in the shell is best if used within two months. If purchased frozen, make sure that the lobster is thoroughly frozen, and return it to the freezer as quickly as possible after purchase. If thawing occurs, cook the lobster right away.

Thaw frozen lobster in the refrigerator for 12 to 24 hours or under cold running water. Lobster that is partially frozen can be prepared without thawing, but a little longer cooking time is required.

Cleaning a lobster requires the same process whether it is boiled or raw. Lay the lobster on its back. With a sharp knife, cut the lobster in half lengthwise. Remove the stomach, which is in the body above the tail, and the intestinal vein, which runs from the stomach to the tip of the tail. Rinse and clean the body cavity thoroughly. If uncooked, the lobster is now ready for baking. If the lobster is boiled and the meat needs to be removed from the shell, use a sharp knife to loosen meat from the edges of the shell. With a fork, pierce the meat at the tip of the tail, lift upward, and pull the meat toward the head and away from the shell.

Crusty Lobster Turnovers

1 cup cooked lobster
2 3-oz. packages cream cheese, softened
2 tbsp. butter, melted
3 tbsp. chopped green onions
⅛ tsp. white pepper
1 8-oz. package refrigerated crescent
   dinner rolls

Preheat oven to 350 degrees. Cut cooked lobster into ½-inch pieces. In a large bowl, thoroughly combine cream cheese and butter. Add lobster, green onions, and white pepper; mix well, being careful to not break up the lobster chunks. Separate crescent rolls into 4 squares. Spoon lobster mixture onto the center of each square. Bring the corners of each square together, forming a triangle shape. Seal seams of the dough. Place on a lightly greased cookie sheet. Bake for 15 to 20 minutes or until golden and puffy. Serves 4.

Crusty Lobster Turnovers

Boiled Lobster

3 qts. water
3 tbsp. salt
2 1-lb., uncooked lobsters, thawed if frozen
Clarified butter, for serving

In a 6-quart saucepan, bring water and salt to a boil. Plunge live lobster head first (or place thawed lobster) into boiling water. Cover and return to the boiling point. Reduce heat and simmer for 12 to 15 minutes (larger lobsters may require a longer cooking time). Drain. Rinse with cold water for 1 to 2 minutes. Split and clean lobster. Serve with clarified butter. Serves 2.

Variations:

To cook frozen lobster tails only, increase salt to ½ cup for 6 5-8 oz. lobster tails. Reduce cooking time to 5 to 10 minutes, depending on the size. Drain. Rinse in cold water for 1 minute. Cut in half lengthwise and serve with clarified butter.

To heat cold, cooked lobster, steam just long enough to heat. If the cooked lobster is frozen, thaw, clean, and rinse the body cavity thoroughly. Place whole lobster or lobster tails on a rack in a covered saucepan or steamer containing a small amount of boiling water. Do not immerse rack in water. Steam just long enough to heat lobster meat thoroughly. Serve immediately in the shell with clarified butter, if desired.

Note: Although broiling cooked lobster is a common practice, steaming is the preferred method for heating cold, cooked lobster because steaming retains the natural moisture and delicate texture of the meat.

Oysters

One of nature's richest sources of iron is the oyster of the northern gulf. Oysters also are high in other minerals, essential vitamins, and protein.

Since some waters are not of sufficient quality to produce edible oysters, exercise extreme caution in gathering your own. This means that you should check with local authorities to determine whether oysters are edible from waters where you plan to search. If buying fresh oysters, always deal with reputable dealers and check with local authorities if you have any questions.

Oysters are marketed in the shell, fresh or frozen, and shucked, frozen, breaded, or canned. Unfrozen oysters must be alive when purchased in the shell, which is indicated by shells that close tightly when handled. Live oysters are sold by the dozen or by the bag, generally in the quantity of a bushel. Oysters will remain alive for seven to ten days after being harvested if refrigerated at 35 to 40 degrees.

Shucked oysters are graded and sold according to size, usually in pints or gallons. The largest shucked oysters are called selects, while the average are called standards. Only on rare occasions will a smaller size, a stewing oyster, or a larger size, a count, be available. Fresh, shucked oysters are plump and have a creamy color and clear liquid. If properly handled and packed in ice, freshly shucked Oysters will maintain quality for about a week. Oysters lose considerable quality during home freezing and should be used only in a casserole or fried upon thawing.

As a result, home freezing of oysters is discouraged, but commercially frozen oysters are fine. The difference is in the quick freezing, not possible with a home freezer. If freezing is necessary, freshly shucked oysters can be frozen in the commercially packed can in which they are bought, or frozen in their own liquor in a container of such size that it will have very little remaining air space when sealed. Use frozen oysters within two months. Cooked oysters should not be frozen at home. Thawing in the refrigerator or in an airtight container under cold running water is acceptable. Once thawed, oysters should not be refrozen.

Some say that three dozen raw oysters in the shell will feed six people. But if you are feeding folks who love raw oysters, a dozen or two per person may be closer to what you need.

To shuck oysters, cotton gloves and an oyster knife are important items to have. An oyster knife has a heavy, metal, wedge-shaped, relatively dull edge blade. The wooden handle is rounded at the end, so it will be comfortable to the hand and, at the same time, withstand the pressure required to open oysters. Don't try to open oysters with a sharp or thin-blade knife. Always rinse the oyster thoroughly before opening. The best way to open an oyster is to hold the oyster by the thin "bill," leaving the hinge (thicker portion) exposed toward the other hand. Usually, there is a small crevice at the hinge. Wearing your cotton gloves (remember, those are important),

1. Insert the oyster knife in the crevice between the shells at the hinge. Twist the knife while pushing it firmly into the opening to slice the hinge.

2. Once the hinge is broken, but before pulling the shell apart, slide the knife along the inside of the top shell and cut the adductor muscle loose from the shell.

3. Remove the top shell and slip the knife under the oyster, being careful not to mutilate the meat, and cut the muscle away from the bottom shell. Remove any remaining shell particles.

Oysters are easy to prepare, and everything inside the shell is edible. They are delicious raw or cooked in a variety of recipes. To preserve the flavor of the oyster and to maintain the natural plumpness and tender quality, cook only long enough to heat thoroughly.

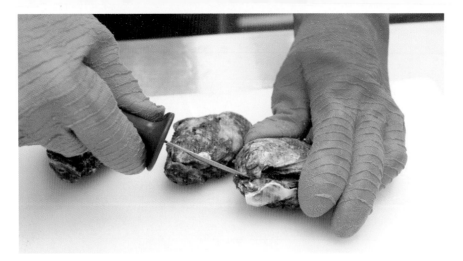

Step 1

Step 2

Step 3

Bacon-Baked Oysters

6 slices bacon, cut into 1-inch pieces
1 cup buttery cracker crumbs, crushed
½ cup mayonnaise
2 tbsp. dehydrated chives
1 tsp. lemon juice
1 tsp. hot sauce
½ tsp. Dijon mustard
4 lbs. rock salt
24 fresh oysters, shucked, with half of the
   shells reserved and cleaned
¼ cup grated Parmesan cheese

Preheat oven to 400 degrees. Partially cook bacon in a 10-inch fry pan until rubbery but not crisp. Set aside. In a small bowl, combine cracker crumbs, mayonnaise, chives, lemon juice, hot sauce, and mustard and mix well. Pour a ½-inch layer of rock salt in a 13x9-inch baking pan. Arrange oysters, each in a half-shell, on the salt until they sit firmly. Top each oyster with crumb mixture; sprinkle with Parmesan cheese. Place a piece of bacon on top of each oyster. Bake for 8 to 10 minutes, or until oysters are hot and tender. Serves 4 to 6.

Fried Oysters

1 pt. oysters, thawed if frozen
2 eggs
Salt and pepper to taste
⅓ cup flour
2 cups bread crumbs
⅓ cup butter
⅓ cup cooking oil

Drain excess liquid from oysters. Beat together the eggs, salt, and pepper. Dip oysters into egg mixture then into flour. Dip into egg mixture again and roll in bread crumbs. Let stand 5 to 10 minutes. Heat butter and oil in large fry pan over moderate heat. Fry oysters for 5 to 7 minutes or until lightly browned, turning once during cooking. Drain on absorbent paper. Serve with a favorite dipping sauce. Serves 6.

Oysters Rockefeller

Oysters Rockefeller

2 pts. oysters, thawed if frozen
½ cup chopped celery
½ cup chopped green onion
¼ cup chopped parsley
½ cup plus 2 tbsp. butter, divided
10 oz. spinach, chopped, defrosted if frozen
2 tbsp. anisette
½ tsp. salt
Rock salt
½ cup dry bread crumbs

Preheat oven to 450 degrees. Drain any excess liquid from the oysters and remove any remaining pieces of shell particles. In a 1-quart saucepan, cook celery, green onion, and parsley in ½ cup butter until tender. Add spinach, anisette, and salt to celery mixture; stir to combine. Place vegetable mixture in a blender or food processor. Blend or process until vegetables are almost puréed. Place a layer of rock salt in 6 pie pans. Place 6 oyster shells or baking shells on top of salt in pans. Place the oysters in the shells. Top each oyster with spinach mixture. Melt remaining 2 tbsp. butter; combine with bread crumbs. Sprinkle on top of spinach mixture. Bake for 10 minutes in the oven. Serve immediately. Serves 12 as an appetizer or 6 as an entrée.

Note: This famed recipe is said to have been created in 1899 by Jules Alciatore, son of the founder of Antoine's restaurant in New Orleans. It was named after America's richest man at the time, John D. Rockefeller. The original recipe was kept secret, but through the years a number of versions have appeared, all similar to the original. This is not the original, nor do we have the exact make-up of the original dish, but this is a good unofficial version.

Scalloped Oysters

1 pt. oysters, thawed if frozen
2 cups cracker crumbs
½ cup butter, melted
½ tsp. salt
⅛ tsp. pepper
¼ tsp. Worcestershire sauce
1 cup milk

Preheat oven to 350 degrees. Drain any excess liquid from the oysters and remove any remaining shell particles. In a medium-sized bowl, combine cracker crumbs, butter, salt, and pepper. Sprinkle ⅓ of crumb mixture in the bottom of a well-greased 1-quart casserole dish. Cover with a layer of oysters. Repeat with one layer of crumbs and one layer of oysters. In a separate dish, add Worcestershire sauce to milk; pour over oysters. Sprinkle remaining crumb mixture on top. Bake for 30 minutes or until brown. Serves 6.

Oysters en Creole Sauce

1 15½-oz. can oysters, thawed if frozen
¼ cup chopped onion
¼ cup chopped green pepper
1 tbsp. chopped fresh parsley
1 clove garlic, finely chopped
¼ cup butter
3 tbsp. all-purpose flour
1 tsp. chili powder
½ tsp. salt
¼ tsp. white pepper
2 medium tomatoes, peeled, seeded, and
   chopped
1 cup tomato puree
2 cups rice, cooked according to package
   directions

Drain oysters and remove any shell particles. Cook onion, green pepper, parsley, and garlic in butter until tender; blend in flour, chili powder, salt, and pepper. Add tomatoes and tomato puree; cook until thickened, stirring constantly. Add oysters and simmer 15 minutes or until the edges of each oyster begin to curl. Serve each portion with ½ cup hot rice. Serves 4.

Oysters on the Grill

As many oysters on the half-shell as you can
   eat
Melted butter
Grated cheese

Place oysters, in the half-shell, on a grill over hot charcoal. Pour butter over each oyster, then sprinkle with cheese. Once the oysters begin to curl, eat the oysters right out of the shells on the grill or transfer the shells to a platter and serve.

Note: This recipe is its most basic form, but it comes in enough versions to fill a book. Put anything on top of the oysters as they heat on the grill and it works. Bacon is a favorite to add, a little piece on top of each oyster, as is almost any commercial seafood seasoning that you can find at the store. Garlic powder always goes well, as does Worcestershire sauce and whatever cheese that you like. One delicious variation is to mix butter with equal parts Worcestershire sauce. Parmesan cheese is a popular choice for your cheese selection.

Rock Shrimp

Rock shrimp tails could easily be mistaken for miniature lobster tails. Deriving its name from the extremely tough, rigid exoskeleton, rock shrimp was, for centuries, the prized catch of fishermen but little known to the public. The hard shell and texture of the meat is like that of a lobster, while the flavor is between that of lobster and shrimp.

This creature is far more perishable than either the northern gulf lobsters or its shrimp relatives. Therefore, most rock shrimp are marketed to be frozen raw as either whole or split tails. Unlike most seafood, which is better purchased fresh, rock shrimp are just as good—and quite often better—when purchased frozen. Rock shrimp are purchased according to size, with the largest at a count of about twenty-one to twenty-five shrimp per pound. Whether purchasing rock shrimp tails, fresh or frozen, the quality can be determined by the shrimp's odor and flesh color. Fresh rock shrimp will have transparent white flesh with no discoloration. The odor of fresh rock shrimp will be mild, with no "off" or objectionable odor. Cleaned and cooked rock shrimp yield about half the weight of the green tails.

Split tails are the easiest to prepare. Cleaning an unsplit tail isn't hard, but you may get nicked up by the hard shell if you don't wear rubber gloves. Thaw the rock shrimp under cold running water as they are being cleaned. Cook them immediately. Cooked rock shrimp maintain quality two to three days in the refrigerator, but raw ones lose quality rapidly, even when refrigerated.

To clean an unsplit tail, hold the tail section in one hand with the swimmerettes facing your palm and the end of the tail near your fingers. Using kitchen shears, insert one blade of the scissors in the sand-vein opening and cut through the shell along the outer curve to the end of the tail. Pull the sides of the shell apart and remove the meat. Wash in cold water to remove the sand vein.

Rock shrimp are quite tasty when broiled in the shell. However, you need to clean them a bit differently. To clean the whole rock shrimp tails for broiling, place a rock shrimp tail on a cutting board with the swimmerettes exposed. With a sharp knife, make a cut between the swimmerettes through the meat to the shell. Spread the shell until it lies flat; wash in cold water to remove the sand vein. Commercially split tails are in this form. The meat can be removed from the shell and either simmered for 25 to 30 seconds or broiled.

Rock shrimp cook faster than other shrimp and require close attention to avoid overcooking. When overcooked, the meat becomes rubbery and unpleasant. To simmer approximately one and a half pounds raw, peeled, and deveined rock shrimp, add 2 tbsp. salt to 1 qt. water and bring to a boil. Place rock shrimp in boiling water and simmer for 30 to 45 seconds. Drain and remove any remaining particles of the sand vein. Serve with melted butter or sauce or use in recipes calling for cooked shrimp. Cooked rock shrimp are also good to use in recipes calling for lobster.

To broil, lay rock shrimp flat on a baking pan with meat exposed. Brush with melted butter. Sprinkle with garlic salt and paprika. Broil 4 inches from the heat source for approximately 2 minutes, or until tails curl at the ends.

Broiled Rock Shrimp

2½ lbs. raw rock shrimp, split and deveined
½ cup butter, melted
¾ tsp. salt
¼ tsp. white pepper
¼ tsp. paprika
Lemon butter

Lemon Butter

½ cup butter, melted
2 tbsp. lemon juice

Lay unfrozen rock shrimp flat on a broiler pan with meat exposed. Baste with butter. Sprinkle with salt, white pepper, and paprika. Broil 4 inches from the heat source for approximately 2 minutes or until meat is opaque. Serve immediately with lemon butter. Serves 6.

Combine butter and lemon juice. Heat until warmed through. Makes approximately ½ cup sauce.

Deviled Rock Shrimp

1 lb. cooked rock shrimp, peeled and
   deveined
1½ cups soft bread crumbs
1 cup milk
1 egg, well beaten
1 tsp. dry mustard
½ tsp. salt
Dash cayenne pepper
½ cup saltine crackers, coarsely crumbled
¼ cup butter, melted, or cooking oil
Parsley, for garnish

Preheat oven to 400 degrees. Cut unfrozen rock shrimp in half. Combine rock shrimp, bread crumbs, milk, egg, dry mustard, salt, and cayenne pepper. Spoon mixture into 6 well-greased 6-oz. custard cups. Combine cracker crumbs with melted butter and sprinkle over the top of the shrimp mixture. Bake for 6 to 8 minutes or until crumbs are browned. Garnish with parsley. Serves 6.

Rock Shrimp Dreams

½ lb. cooked rock shrimp, peeled and
   deveined
6 oz. cream cheese, softened
½ cup chopped pecans
½ cup crushed pineapple, drained
¼ cup olives, chopped
1 tbsp. lime juice
6 slices white bread, lightly buttered
6 slices wheat bread, lightly buttered

Chop rock shrimp into medium-size pieces. Place shrimp in a bowl; add cream cheese, pecans, pineapple, olives, and lime juice and mix well. Spread equal amounts of shrimp mixture on 6 slices of white bread; cover with remaining slices of wheat bread. Cut each sandwich diagonally into 4 pieces. Serves 4.

Rock Shrimp Étouffée

¼ cup butter, melted
3 tbsp. all-purpose flour
1 cup chopped onion
½ cup chopped celery
¼ cup chopped green pepper
2 tbsp. chopped parsley
1 clove garlic, minced
½ cup water
2 lbs. cooked rock shrimp, peeled and
   deveined
1 tbsp. lemon juice
¼ tsp. salt
¼ tsp. cayenne pepper
3 cups rice, cooked according to package
   directions

In a 10-inch skillet, combine butter and flour. Add onion, celery, green pepper, parsley, and garlic. Cook over medium heat for 5 minutes or until vegetables are tender, stirring constantly. Add water gradually, still stirring, and continue to cook until thick. Stir in rock shrimp, lemon juice, salt, and cayenne pepper. Continue to cook until shrimp are heated through. Serve over rice. Serves 6.

Rock Shrimp with Linguine

1 lb. raw rock shrimp, peeled and deveined,
    thawed if frozen
1 cup sliced fresh mushrooms
¼ cup chopped green onions
1 clove garlic, crushed
⅓ cup butter
3 tbsp. all-purpose flour
1 tsp. salt
¾ cup dry white wine
2 cups half-and-half
⅓ cup chopped parsley
4 to 6 servings of linguine, cooked according
    to package directions
Grated Parmesan cheese, optional

Sauté rock shrimp, mushrooms, green onions, and garlic in butter over low heat for 1 to 2 minutes. Blend in flour and salt; mix well. Stir in wine. Gradually add half-and-half, stirring constantly to form a smooth sauce. Add chopped parsley. Simmer for 3 minutes. Toss with linguine and sprinkle with Parmesan cheese, if desired. Serves 4 to 6.

Rock Shrimp Stir-Fry with Crunchy Vegetables

2 tbsp. vegetable oil
1½ lbs. raw rock shrimp, peeled and deveined,
    thawed if frozen
½ cup thinly sliced green onion
2 cloves garlic, minced
1 cup boiling water
1 tsp. instant chicken broth
10 oz. fresh or frozen broccoli, chopped
9 oz. fresh or frozen French-style green beans
4 oz. mushrooms, sliced, drained if canned
1 tsp. ginger
2 tbsp. soy sauce
1 tbsp. cornstarch

Heat oil in a 12-inch skillet or wok. Add rock shrimp, green onion, and garlic; stir-fry for 3 minutes. Add water and instant chicken broth; stir to dissolve. Add broccoli, green beans, mushrooms, and ginger. Cover; bring to a boil. Reduce heat; simmer for 6 minutes or until vegetables are tender but crisp, separating vegetables with a fork after 2 or 3 minutes. In a small bowl, combine soy sauce and cornstarch; stir into rock shrimp mixture. Cook over medium heat, stirring constantly until sauce thickens. Serves 6.

Scallops

The scallop is a bivalve shellfish, but unlike the stationary oyster, actively swims in the many grass beds in bays of the northern gulf. The scallop swims by squirting water through its shell. This causes the adductor muscle to grow extremely large and extremely edible—in fact, it is the only part that is eaten.

If you gather your own scallops, you will be gathering bay scallops. Because of heavy harvesting and other factors, only a few areas are open for recreational harvesting. In addition, there typically are harvesting seasons and other regulations. Check with local authorities before gathering scallops. Most recreational scallop gathering is done by waders or snorkelers who sight the scallops in or around grass beds. When they see a scallop, they simply reach down and pick it up. Scallops should be shucked immediately after being taken from the water and the meat iced.

When buying scallops in the market, examine the meat for a creamy white, light tan, or pinkish color and a slightly sweet odor. If purchased in packages, fresh or frozen, scallops should be practically free of liquid. Fresh scallops should be stored on ice in a refrigerator between 35 and 40 degrees. They should be used the day of purchase if possible, but can be held on ice for up to two days.

Raw, frozen scallops can be held at 0 degrees or below for three to four months. Thaw frozen scallops in the refrigerator or under cold running water. After thawing, raw scallops should have the slightly sweet odor characteristic of other fresh seafood.

To shuck a scallop, hold it in the palm of one hand with the shell's hinge against the palm and the "bill" extending toward the opposite hand.

1. Insert a slender-bladed knife between the halves of the shell near the hinge, then twist the knife to pry the shell apart. Some scallop shuckers use a thin spoon for this, because the spoon's curve fits with the shell's curve.

2. Lift the top side of the shell far enough to insert the knife point, and slice the muscle from the top of the shell. Remove the top shell.

3. Clean out all the viscera (everything that does not look like a muscle).

4. Cut the muscle from the bottom shell. Rinse the meat in cold water and ice immediately.

Creamy Orzo with Scallops, Asparagus, and Parmesan

1 lb. scallops
5 tbsp. butter, divided
½ cup diced yellow onion
4 to 6 quarts water
1 lb. orzo pasta
1 cup asparagus, cut into 1-inch pieces
½ cup grated Parmesan cheese
½ cup heavy whipping cream
1 tbsp. fresh parsley, chopped, plus more for
    garnish
½ tsp. salt
Freshly ground black pepper, to taste

Rinse scallops and pat dry. Set aside. Melt 1 tbsp. of the butter in a large skillet over medium heat. Add the onion and sauté until soft, about 4 to 5 minutes. Remove the onion to a plate and set aside. Next, add 2 tbsp. of the butter to the skillet and melt over medium heat. Add the prepared scallops and sauté for 4 to 5 minutes, then remove scallops from the pan, place on a heated platter, and cover with foil. Fill a pot with water and bring to a boil. Add the orzo and stir. After the orzo has been boiling for 5 minutes, add the asparagus and continue to cook for 5 additional minutes. Once the orzo and asparagus are cooked and tender, drain well and pour into a large mixing bowl. Quickly add the Parmesan cheese and the final 2 tbsp. butter to the orzo and asparagus mixture. Stir thoroughly, allowing both the cheese and butter to melt. Slowly add the cream, stirring constantly. Next, add the sautéed onions, scallops, and fresh parsley. Mix well. Season with salt and pepper. Garnish with additional parsley. Serve immediately. Serves 4.

Note: Photographer Celeste Ward says, "This recipe is a family favorite and is easy, delicious, and incredibly comforting. Fresh, sautéed bay scallops are the star of this dish. The creamy orzo pairs perfectly with the satisfying crunch of the asparagus, and the addition of grated Parmesan cheese rounds it out wonderfully."

Fried Scallops

2 lbs. scallops, thawed if frozen
1 tsp. salt
2 cups cracker meal or saltine crackers, finely
    crushed
Oil for frying

Rinse scallops with cold water. Drain and sprinkle with salt. Roll scallops in cracker meal; coat well. Fry in oil at approximately 350 degrees for 3 to 5 minutes or until done. Rest on paper towels to remove excess oil. Serves 6.

Creamy Orzo with Scallops,
Asparagus, and Parmesan

Broiled Scallops

2 lbs. scallops, thawed if frozen
½ cup butter
¾ tsp. to 1 tsp. garlic, minced
½ tsp. salt
⅛ tsp. pepper
Paprika to taste

Rinse scallops with cold water. Melt butter in small saucepan. Add garlic and cook over very low heat for 5 minutes; do not brown. Place scallops in a single layer in an 11x7-inch baking dish. Sprinkle scallops with salt and pepper. Pour garlic butter over scallops, being sure to coat on all sides. Broil about 4 inches from source of heat for 2 minutes. Turn scallops; broil 2 minutes longer. Sprinkle with paprika. Serve immediately. Serves 6.

Note: Some versions of this popular recipe include 2 tbsp. lemon juice and white pepper instead of black pepper.

Honey-Broiled Scallops

1 lb. scallops
3 tbsp. lime juice
2 tbsp. vegetable oil
1 tbsp. honey
1 tbsp. soy sauce
¼ tsp. ground ginger
¼ cup sesame seeds, toasted, optional

Rinse scallops to remove any remaining shell particles. In a 2-quart mixing bowl, combine lime juice, oil, honey, soy sauce, and ginger. Add scallops and mix until well coated. Cover and chill for 3 to 6 hours, stirring frequently. Remove scallops from marinade, reserving marinade. Thread scallops evenly on 4 skewers. Broil 4 inches from source of heat for 3 to 5 minutes or until opaque throughout, turning occasionally and basting with reserved marinade. If desired, place sesame seeds on waxed paper and roll each skewer over the seeds to evenly coat scallops. Serves 4.

Sautéed Scallops

1 lb. scallops
¼ cup butter
1 clove garlic, minced
2 tbsp. chives
Splash of white wine

Melt butter in skillet; add garlic and chives. Add scallops and stir gently until the meat becomes opaque. Pour wine over scallops and stir for 1 to 2 minutes. Serves 3 to 4.

Scallop Gazpacho

1½ lbs. cooked scallops
4 cups tomato juice
½ cup Worcestershire sauce
½ cup chopped red bell pepper
½ cup chopped green bell pepper
1 tsp. liquid hot sauce
1 tsp. lemon juice

In a large mixing bowl, combine all ingredients; mix well. Pour into a serving bowl and cover tightly. Refrigerate for several hours or overnight. Serve cold. Serves 6.

Note: Gazpacho recipes come in a number of variations. Other additions that you may wish to include are: small diced cucumbers, diced tomatillos, diced green onions, chopped celery, and/or a tablespoon of red wine vinegar. Some cooks substitute the red bell pepper with roasted red pepper. Others add shrimp for a more varied seafood flavor. This recipe is easily customizable to your preferences and taste buds.

Scallops with Peaches

1 lb. scallops
2 tbsp. butter
2 tbsp. lemon juice
¾ tsp. salt, divided
Dash pepper
12 canned peach halves
¼ tsp. cinnamon
¼ tsp. cloves
¼ tsp. mace
3 slices bacon

Combine scallops, butter, lemon juice, ½ tsp. salt, and pepper in a microwave-safe dish. Cover and cook in microwave on high for 2 minutes. Drain peach halves and place cut side up on another microwave-safe dish. Combine cinnamon, cloves, mace, and ¼ tsp. salt; sprinkle over peaches. Place scallop mixture evenly in the center of each peach half. Cut bacon crosswise in fourths; place a piece on each peach. Cook, uncovered, in microwave on high for 6 to 7 minutes; rotate dish once during cooking. Serves 6.

Shrimp

Shrimp is one of the most popular shellfish in the United States, thanks to its distinctive flavor and tender and delicate pale meat.

The shrimp is a ten-legged crustacean that wears its skeleton on the outside. There are a multitude of different kinds of shrimp, but those most commonly found in fresh markets are the white, brown, and pink harvested from the warm waters of the northern Gulf of Mexico. They are interchangeable in any shrimp recipe and may have a slightly different color when raw, but that is only cosmetic. Each cooks and tastes just like the others. There are two shrimp species that differ from their siblings. First, the royal red is a bright red shrimp caught in extremely deep water off the northern gulf coast. Some say that its flavor reminds them of lobster. It is a highly sought-after species and available in the region's fresh markets. Second, rock shrimp also are a warm-water species, but are handled differently than other shrimp. These are discussed in a separate section.

"Green" shrimp is a term used to describe raw shrimp of any kind still in the shell. Regardless of the color of the green shrimp, when cooked, the shells of all species turn red, the meat becomes white with reddish tinges, and the flavor and nutritional value remain the same.

Shrimp usually are sold according to size based on the number of headless shrimp per pound; the categories generally are differentiated as jumbo, large, medium, and small, with jumbo indicating fifteen or fewer shrimp per pound and small, sixty or more per pound.

Roughly speaking, two pounds of raw, headless, unpeeled shrimp, properly cooked, will yield one pound of cooked, peeled, and deveined shrimp.

The cleaning method is the same for raw or cooked shrimp, but it is easier to do when raw:

1. To peel, hold the tail of the shrimp in one hand. Slip thumb of other hand under the shell between swimmerettes, and lift off several segments of shell. Repeat, if necessary, removing all but the tail section.

2. If tail section is to be removed, hold the shell section and squeeze with thumb and forefinger. Pull the shrimp meat with the other hand until it is released from the shell.

3. The vein (often black) located along the upper curve of the body is commonly referred to as the "sand vein." Some people prefer to remove it in order to prevent any sand or grit in the cooked shrimp. It can be removed before or after cooking, but is easier to remove before cooking. The vein is part of the circulatory system (not the intestine, as some folks joke) and need not be removed. To remove the sand vein, make a cut with a sharp knife about ⅛-inch deep along the upper curve of the shrimp. Rinse away the sand vein under cold water.

There are several types of shrimp peeling and deveining tools on the market. Some work better than others, but all are designed to remove the shell and vein from the shrimp in one easy motion. All work best when shrimp are raw.

Shrimp may be prepared in hundreds of ways and served as almost any course in a menu. Shrimp are an excellent source of high-quality protein, vitamins, and minerals, and because they are low in calories and easy to digest, they fit into many diets.

If all you want from your market are unpeeled boiled or steamed shrimp, and if you don't mind dealing with the sand vein after the shrimp is cooked, let the market do the cooking. Most markets offer free or inexpensive steaming of purchased shrimp. They have it down to a science—steamed just the right amount, ready to peel and eat, no spices to buy or pots to clean.

In terms of "fresh" shrimp, except for the small-boat day shrimpers who bring their catch to the dock each day, most commercial shrimpers quick-freeze their catch shortly after they drag it up out of the water. So, if you are buying "fresh" shrimp in a market, it probably means that you are buying shrimp that has recently been thawed. That isn't a bad thing, however. The shrimp flavor and texture does not change. In fact, it may be better for the consumer, because shrimp thawed in small quantities that can be sold within hours after thawing will have a higher quality than unfrozen (or even fresh) shrimp that has laid around in a display case for several days. While it may not feel the same as buying "fresh" shrimp, purchasing shrimp still frozen is an excellent option.

If you are dead set on buying never-frozen, fresh shrimp, scout out docks where the day-shrimpers keep their boats and find out when they usually get to the dock each day. It probably will be in the morning. Many day shrimpers will gladly sell their catch directly to you, because it allows them to get a higher price than selling their catch to a market at a wholesale rate. The downside to this option is that you often will have to buy whatever the shrimper has just caught, which can range from small to jumbo shrimp. Day shrimpers often don't take time to carefully grade the shrimp while on the water—why would they? On the water, their job is to catch the shrimp, not grade them. So even if you tell the shrimper that you want mediums, you may get some smalls and jumbos mixed in.

A market may be an easier prospect to select and buy your shrimp, but it can be fun hanging around a dock, watching the watermen do their work and buying the absolute freshest and unfrozen seafood available. So, if you have the time and inclination, go for the adventure—and get some delicious shrimp while you're at it.

Alternatively, certain individuals will try to catch their own shrimp, and a few of them succeed. Some boat-owning coastal residents will purchase small nets (miniatures of what the big shrimpers use) to drag behind their boats to catch shrimp. If they know what they are doing and where to go, they can catch enough shrimp for a family feast or several feasts. Others look for shrimp with circular cast nets, the same nets that fishermen use to catch bait minnows. Shrimp can be found just about anywhere. In the gulf. Bays. Saltwater creeks. Lagoons. They tend to sit on the bottom, waiting for a shrimper's net to scoop them up. A person with a throw net need only to start throwing and see what gets dragged in. One old, retired fellow in Gulf Shores, Alabama, discovered a spot where a stream flowed into the Intracoastal Waterway just east of Bon Secour Bay. Whenever he wanted shrimp for dinner, he motored down to the spot, cast the net for a while, and came back home with enough shrimp for him and his wife. That doesn't always happen. Many times, the shrimp are nowhere to be found. But if you want to have a little fun, give it a try. The worst that can happen is that you have to detour by the fish market on the way home.

½ cup chili sauce
1 tbsp. lemon juice
½ cup ketchup
2 tsp. horseradish

Combine all ingredients in a small bowl. Chill. Makes approximately 1 cup sauce.

Or, if you're looking for something a little jazzier, try this instead.

¾ cup ketchup
1 tsp. Worcestershire sauce
2 tbsp. lemon juice
¼ tsp. salt
1 tbsp. grated onion
⅛ tsp. pepper

Combine all ingredients in a small bowl. Chill. Makes approximately ¾ cup sauce.

Note: One of the most popular ways to eat shrimp is boiled and dipped in a cocktail sauce. These recipes taste great and are easy for vacationers to mix up quickly.

# Shrimp Creole

1½ lbs. boiled shrimp, peeled and deveined
1 cup chopped onion
1 cup celery
1 cup chopped bell pepper
1 tbsp. garlic, minced
2 tbsp. bacon drippings
1 tbsp. Worcestershire sauce
1 tsp. salt
½ tsp. pepper
Hot sauce to taste
1 qt. fresh tomatoes, chopped
6-8 servings rice, cooked according to
    package directions

Preheat oven to 450 degrees. Sauté shrimp, onion, celery, bell pepper, and garlic in bacon drippings. Add Worcestershire sauce, salt, pepper, hot sauce, and tomatoes, and place into a 2½-quart baking dish. Bake for 15 minutes. Remove from oven and serve over rice. Serves 6 to 8.

Note: There is no end to the variations of Shrimp Creole. For some, it is shrimp in a tomato-based sauce over rice. For others, it contains few vegetables other than the holy trinity. This basic recipe is a relatively quick and easy version.

Depending on how much time and how many ingredients you want include, some people add 1 tbsp. Creole seasoning, 1 tbsp. tomato paste, ¼ cup dry white wine, 1 bay leaf, fresh thyme, or green onion tops, thinly sliced. You can add any or all, whichever flavors you like.

Boiled Shrimp

2 lbs. raw, headless, shrimp, thawed if frozen,
   peeled and deveined
2 tbsp. salt
5 cups water

Rinse shrimp thoroughly and drain. Add salt to water and bring to a boil. Add shrimp and reduce heat. Cover and simmer 3 to 4 minutes or until the largest shrimp is opaque in the center when tested by cutting in half; drain. Serve warm or cold with cocktail sauce. Makes approximately 1 lb. cooked, peeled, and deveined shrimp.

Note: Cooking time will vary according to size of shrimp.

For more flavor, squeeze the juice of two lemons into the water before boiling, and drop the lemons in too. Also, commercial shrimp boil, available at grocery stores and fish markets, can be added to the water, if desired.

Shrimp Kabobs

4 slices bacon, cut into 1-inch squares
1½ lbs. raw shrimp, peeled and deveined,
   thawed if frozen
4 oz. mushrooms, drained if canned
1 green pepper, cut into 1-inch squares
3 tbsp. butter, melted, or cooking oil
½ tsp. salt
Dash pepper

Partially cook bacon until rubbery but not crisp. Place a shrimp, a bacon square, a mushroom, and a green pepper square on a short skewer. Place kabobs on a well-greased broiler pan. In a small bowl, combine butter, salt, and pepper; brush onto kabobs. Broil, about 3 inches from heat source, for 5 minutes. Turn kabobs and baste with butter mixture. Broil for an additional 3 to 5 minutes. Makes approximately 24 kabobs.

Jambalaya

2 tbsp. butter
¾ cup chopped onion
½ cup chopped celery
¼ cup chopped green pepper
1 tbsp. chopped parsley
1 clove garlic, minced
2 cups cubed, fully-cooked ham
1 28-oz. can tomatoes, undrained and
  chopped
1 10½-oz. can beef broth
10½ oz. water
1 cup uncooked long-grain rice
1 tsp. sugar
½ tsp. thyme
½ tsp. chili powder
¼ tsp. pepper
1½ lbs. raw shrimp, peeled and deveined,
  thawed if frozen

Melt butter in a Dutch oven. Add onion, celery, green pepper, parsley, and garlic. Cover and cook until tender. Add ham, tomatoes, beef broth, water, rice, sugar, thyme, chili powder, and pepper. Cover and simmer for 25 minutes or until rice is tender. Add shrimp. Simmer, uncovered, until shrimp are cooked and sauce reaches a desired consistency, about 5 to 10 minutes. Serves 6 to 8.

Note: To measure the water, fill up the can from the beef broth 1 time.

Stuffed Shrimp

2 lbs. raw jumbo shrimp (approximately 24 to 30), peeled except for the end of the tail, deveined, thawed if frozen
¾ tsp. salt, divided
2 tsp. butter
¼ cup finely chopped onion
2 tbsp. finely chopped green onion
2 tbsp. finely chopped celery
2 tbsp. finely chopped green pepper
1 tbsp. chopped parsley
1 clove garlic, minced
6½-7 oz. crab meat, drained if canned, flaked, and cartilage removed
¼ tsp. cayenne pepper
2 eggs, beaten
1 5½-oz. can evaporated milk
1 cup all-purpose flour
3 cups soft white bread crumbs
Oil for deep frying

Butterfly the shrimp by cutting along their outside curve about ¾ of the way through; carefully flatten. Sprinkle with ¼ tsp. salt. In small saucepan, melt butter. Add onion, green onion, celery, green pepper, parsley and garlic. Cover and cook 5 minutes or until tender. Remove from heat. Stir in crabmeat, ½ tsp. salt, and cayenne pepper. Pack stuffing mixture in a band down the center of each shrimp, dividing it equally among them. Combine eggs and evaporated milk in a shallow bowl. Place flour and bread crumbs on separate plates. One at a time, roll the shrimp in the flour to coat evenly, dip into egg mixture, then roll in bread crumbs. Arrange on a baking sheet and refrigerate for 1 hour to firm up the coating. Arrange 5 or 6 shrimp in a single layer in a fry basket. Fry in oil heated to 350 degrees for 3 to 5 minutes, or until shrimp are brown and cooked through. Drain on absorbent paper. Keep warm in a very low oven while remaining shrimp are being cooked. Serves 6.

Shrimp Pilau

3 slices bacon, cut into small pieces
1 cup chopped green pepper
¼ cup chopped onion
¾ cup water
1 14½-oz. can whole tomatoes
¾ cup uncooked rice
1 tsp. salt
⅛ tsp. pepper
⅛ tsp. thyme
1 lb. raw shrimp, peeled and deveined

In a 2-quart saucepan, cook bacon until crisp. Remove bacon from pan and cook green pepper and onion in bacon fat until tender. Add water and tomatoes and bring it to a boil. Stir in rice, salt, pepper, and thyme. Reduce heat to low, cover, and cook for 18 to 20 minutes. Mix in shrimp, cover, and continue cooking for 10 to 12 minutes or until shrimp are tender, being careful not to overcook the shrimp. Garnish with bacon. Serves 6.

Roasted Greek Shrimp with Orzo

Roasted Greek Shrimp with Orzo

1 lb. shrimp, peeled, deveined, with tails on
1 2¼-oz. can sliced olives, drained
5 oz. grape tomatoes, halved
1 tbsp. chopped fresh parsley, plus more for
   garnish
6 oz. quartered and marinated artichoke
   hearts, drained
2 tbsp. extra virgin olive oil, divided
⅛ tsp. garlic salt
Freshly ground black pepper to taste, divided
1 cup orzo pasta
1 tsp. lemon zest
Salt to taste
½ cup feta cheese, crumbled

Preheat the oven to 400 degrees. Place the shrimp in a large mixing bowl. Add the olives, grape tomatoes, and fresh parsley. Squeeze all excess liquid out of the artichoke hearts and add to the bowl. Drizzle 1 tbsp. extra virgin olive oil over the mixture and season with the garlic salt and freshly ground black pepper. Stir well to thoroughly combine the ingredients. Spread the mixture in a single layer on a baking sheet lined with a silicone baking mat or parchment paper. Roast in the pre-heated oven for approximately 10 to 12 minutes, or until the shrimp are cooked through. While the shrimp mixture is roasting, cook orzo according to package directions; drain. Drizzle with remaining 1 tbsp. extra virgin olive oil. Add lemon zest. Season with salt and pepper; stir to combine. Place shrimp on top of the orzo mixture. Sprinkle with feta cheese and garnish with fresh parsley. Serves 4.

Note: This recipe, created by the photographer, Celeste Ward, will quickly become one of your new favorites. It is packed with vibrant flavors that will leave your taste buds singing. Plus, it's very easy to make and is ready in just minutes!

Shrimp Scampi

½ cup butter
¾ cup olive oil
3 cloves garlic, crushed
2 tbsp. parsley
½ cup dry white wine or vermouth
1 tsp. basil
2 tbsp. fresh lemon juice
1 lb. raw shrimp, peeled and deveined
Cooked rice, for serving

Melt butter. Add olive oil, garlic, parsley, wine, basil, and lemon juice. Simmer for 5 minutes. Place shrimp on a broiler pan. Pour butter mixture over shrimp; broil for 5 to 7 minutes, or until shrimp are cooked. Serve over rice. Serves 4.

Shrimp and Grits

2 cups water
½ cup quick grits
⅛ tsp. salt
⅛ tsp. pepper
4 slices bacon
½ green bell pepper, chopped
½ medium onion, chopped
3 tsp. minced garlic
15 to 20 large shrimp, cooked and deveined
2 tsp. butter
4 green onions, chopped

Bring water to a boil. Add grits, salt, and pepper, and cook. Alternatively, use the directions on the grits' box. While grits are cooking, cook bacon until crispy in a large skillet on medium heat. Remove bacon and crumble, reserving the grease. Cook bell pepper and onion in bacon grease until tender. Add garlic and continue cooking for 1 to 2 minutes. Add shrimp to skillet and cook until heated through. When grits are cooked, mix in butter. Spoon grits onto a plate, then top with shrimp mixture. Garnish with crumbled bacon and chopped green onions. Serves 2 to 3.

Variations:

For creamy grits, some cooks add cream or half-and-half. For this recipe, ½ cup cream will do. Add cream to the pot along with the water.

Cheesy grits are one of the most popular forms. As soon as the grits are removed from the stove, add ⅔ cup shredded cheddar cheese and stir to combine.

Big-time chefs probably would not approve of the use of quick grits. Most chefs prefer regular grits, gourmet stone-ground grits, or polenta instead of quick grits. It really just depends on how much trouble and time you want to go to.

Some enjoy a tomato-ey flavor to the dish and add a 14½-oz. can of diced tomatoes, drained, to the skillet after cooking the pepper and onion but before adding the shrimp.

Replace the bacon with chopped kielbasa sausage or a similar sausage. Cook the sausage until browned and stir into shrimp mixture rather than using as a garnish.

Regarding shrimp, some people like to remove the tails before they go in the pan. That's just fine—the recipe works well either way. Also, raw shrimp can be used just as well as pre-cooked shrimp. Add to the pan per the directions, but allow them to cook until they turn pink and the flesh is opaque. Shrimp cooks rapidly, so be careful not to overcook, which will give the shrimp a rubbery texture.

Note: Since this simple dish first moved off of the breakfast plates of coastal fishermen and onto the menus of restaurants from one end of the northern gulf coast to the other, cooks have developed more variations than you can count. Whatever version you choose, someone will tell you about a different variation and claim it to be the ultimate recipe. Depending on what you prefer, it might be true. With these variations, you can customize this dish to your preference.

Squid

Some folks fish for squid along the northern gulf coast, most often at night. These fishermen understand the comings and goings of squid—when to find them and where. Fisherman often use rigs with multiple small hooks baited with jigs or small natural bait. Few coast visitors go after squid for a couple of reasons. Going after them is a little different than going after finfish. Charter boats don't target squid. Also, many people don't like the idea of putting something in their mouths that is often used as bait for reef fish.

Gulf squid are not the giants that television programs like to feature. They are more tender and smaller in size, rarely exceeding a foot from end to end. Squid can be bought in some fresh markets. For those who don't feel that they are depriving the bait market, these creatures provide a tasty meal.

Perhaps some of the primary questions when it comes to squid are how to clean it and what parts to eat. If you want stuffed squid or squid rings, take a knife and cut through the arms near the eyes. Squeeze out the inedible beak, which you will find near the cut. Feel inside the mantle for the chitinous pen and pull it out. Under cold running water, peel off the speckled membrane that covers the mantle. Wash the mantle thoroughly and drain. It is then ready either for stuffing or cutting into rings. If you want squid in strips slice the mantle lengthwise from top to tail. Spread it open, rinse it thoroughly, and cut into strips. Tentacles can be chopped, minced, or left whole. If the idea eating the tentacles is less than appetizing, discard them as you wish.

Squid in Tomato Sauce

2 lbs. whole squid, thawed if frozen
1 cup sliced onion
1 clove garlic, minced
2 tbsp. butter, melted
1 28-oz. can tomatoes, undrained
½ tsp. basil leaves
¼ cup water
1 tbsp. flour
1 tsp. salt
Cooked hot rice, for serving

Clean squid and cut mantle and tentacles into 1-inch pieces. Cook onion and garlic in butter until vegetables are tender. Add tomatoes and basil; simmer for 5 minutes. Add squid. Cover and bring to a boil. Reduce heat and simmer for 3 to 5 minutes or until squid is tender. Combine water, flour, and salt. Add to squid mixture, stirring constantly, and continue to cook until thick. Serve with cooked rice. Serves 6.

Fried Squid

3 lbs. whole squid, thawed if frozen
3 tbsp. lemon juice
1½ tsp. salt
⅛ tsp. white pepper
2 eggs, beaten
3 tbsp. milk
1½ cups all-purpose flour
Cooking oil, for frying
Lemon wedges, for serving

Clean squid. Cut the mantle crosswise into ½-inch rings. Cut tentacles into 1-inch pieces. Sprinkle lemon juice, salt, and pepper on squid. In a separate bowl, combine egg and milk. Dip squid in egg mixture and roll in flour. Place squid in a single layer in hot oil in a 10-inch frying pan. Fry at approximately 350 degrees for 3 to 5 minutes. Turn carefully. Fry 3 to 5 minutes longer or until squid is lightly browned. Drain excess oil on absorbent paper. Serve with lemon wedges. Serves 6.

Seafood Marinara with Pasta

8 oz. squid
¼ cup chopped onion
2 tbsp. chopped green pepper
1 clove garlic, crushed
2 tbsp. cooking oil
1 8-oz. can tomato sauce
3 oz. tomato paste
½ cup water
1 tsp. sugar
½ tsp. basil
½ tsp. oregano
⅛ tsp. pepper
Cooked pasta, for serving

Clean squid and cut into rings or strips. Cook onion, green pepper, and garlic in hot oil until tender. Add tomato sauce, tomato paste, water, sugar, basil, oregano, and pepper. Cook and simmer for 15 minutes, stirring occasionally. Add squid. Cover and simmer for approximately 5 minutes or until squid is tender. Serve over cooked pasta. Serves 2.

Fried Squid

Amberjack

The amberjack is one of the largest members of the jack family, which has two dozen or more relatives in the Gulf of Mexico. Charter-boat deck hands refer to them as reef mules because of their stubborn and legendary fighting ability. It is a strong fisherman who does not have to sit down for a few minutes after cranking up a large jack from a deep reef.

Jacks are typically long, muscular fish with forked tails. Close amberjack relatives almaco jack, lesser amberjack, and banded rudderfish can be treated in the same way as the amberjack for cooking purposes.

Once considered trash fish, amberjacks have become quite popular in coastal restaurants, particularly when grilled. A Destin, Florida, restaurant contends that it created the first grilled amberjack, and no one has mounted a serious contest to that claim.

These jacks, especially the larger ones, may have clearly visible worms in their flesh. So, if you catch one or buy one whole in the market, keep an eye out for any translucent white material embedded in the flesh. Some of the more genteel among us consider this a bit gross. However, trust me: if you see a worm, trim it out and move on with your recipe—everything will be just fine.

Grilled Amberjack

2 lbs. amberjack fillets, thawed if frozen
1 cup oil-based Italian dressing
2 tsp. salt
½ tsp. oregano

Cut amberjack into serving-size pieces. Place fish in a single layer in a shallow baking dish. Pour Italian dressing over the fish and marinate in refrigerator for at least 30 minutes, overnight if possible, turning once halfway through. Remove fish from dressing and sprinkle with salt and oregano. Place fish on a well-greased grill over hot charcoal. Cook until fish flakes easily when tested with a fork, approximately 10 minutes per inch of thickness. Check doneness frequently so as to not overcook and turn once during grilling. Serves 6.

Note: This is the recipe that pulled Amberjack out of the "trash fish" category and onto restaurant menus from one end of the northern gulf coast to the other.

Grilled Amberjack with Artichoke Mushroom Sauce

2 lbs. amberjack fillets
1 tbsp. lemon juice
2 cups fresh mushrooms, chopped
4 tbsp. butter, divided
3 tbsp. all-purpose flour
1 tsp. salt
1 tsp. white pepper
2 cups heavy whipping cream
3 tbsp. cooking sherry
3 oz. Swiss cheese, chopped
1 tbsp. bacon bits
1 14-oz. can artichoke hearts

Cut amberjack into serving-size portions. Brush fish with lemon juice and grill over medium-hot coals until fish flakes easily with a fork. Set aside; keep warm. Cook mushrooms in 1 tbsp. butter until tender. Remove from pan and set aside. In the same pan, melt the remaining 3 tbsp. butter. Blend in flour, salt, and pepper; add cream, sherry, cheese, and bacon bits. Cook until cheese has melted and sauce is thick, stirring constantly. Add mushrooms and artichokes; heat thoroughly. Serve over fish fillets. Serves 6.

Grilled Amberjack with Artichoke Mushroom Sauce

Amberjack St. Augustine

1½ lbs. amberjack fillets
1 tsp. ground marjoram
1 tsp. ground allspice
1 tsp. pepper
½ tsp. salt
½ tsp. ground thyme
2 tbsp. minced onion
1 tsp. minced garlic

Place fish on a well-oiled broiling pan. In a small bowl, combine marjoram, allspice, pepper, salt, and thyme; apply generously to fish. Mix onion and garlic; spread over fish. Broil 5 to 6 inches from heat source for 15 to 20 minutes or until fish flakes easily with a fork. Serves 4.

Amberjack with Spanish Rice

1 lb. skinless amberjack fillets, thawed if
   frozen
½ cup chopped onion
½ cup chopped green pepper
½ clove garlic, minced
2 tbsp. butter
1 10¾-oz. can condensed tomato soup
1½ cups water
1½ cups quick-cooking rice, uncooked
2 tsp. Worcestershire sauce
4 whole cloves
1 tsp. dry mustard
½ tsp. salt
½ tsp. pepper
Parsley, for garnish

Cut amberjack into 1-inch pieces. In a large skillet, cook onion, green pepper, and garlic in butter until tender. Add tomato soup, water, rice, Worcestershire sauce, cloves, mustard, salt, pepper, and amberjack pieces; mix well. Cook over low heat for 10 to 12 minutes or until liquid is absorbed and fish flakes easily with a fork. Remove cloves. Garnish with parsley. Serves 4 to 6.

Cheese-Crusted Amberjack

2 lbs. amberjack fillets
½ cup herb and garlic salad dressing
½ cup cornflake crumbs
½ cup shredded sharp Cheddar cheese
6 thin orange slices, for garnish

Cut fish into serving-size portions. Place fish in a single layer in a shallow baking dish. Pour dressing over fillets, cover, and marinate in the refrigerator for several hours, turning fish 3 or 4 times. Preheat oven to 450 degrees. Combine cornflake crumbs and cheese in a shallow bowl. Roll fish in crumb mixture, coating thoroughly. Arrange fish in lightly-oiled baking dish; sprinkle with any remaining crumb mixture. Bake for 15 to 20 minutes or until fish flakes easily with a fork. Garnish with orange slices. Serves 6.

Hot Honey Amberjack

1 cup honey
½ cup prepared mustard
1 tsp. white pepper
1 tsp. lemon juice
2 lbs. amberjack steaks, thawed if frozen

Combine honey, mustard, white pepper, and lemon juice in a medium-sized bowl. Baste both sides of amberjack steaks with the honey mixture. Place steaks on a well-greased, hinged wire grill. Cook on both sides for 10 minutes per inch of thickness at about 4 inches from moderately hot coals, basting often until fish flakes easily when tested with a fork. Serves 6.

Lemon Pepper Amberjack

2 lbs. amberjack fillets, thawed if frozen
Juice from 2 lemons
Salt and pepper to taste

Cut amberjack into serving-size pieces. Combine lemon juice, salt, and pepper in a small dish. Place fish on a well-greased grill over hot charcoal and baste liberally with lemon juice mixture. Turn fish and baste. Cook until fish flakes easily when tested with a fork, about 10 minutes per inch of thickness. Serves 6.

Note: This is an even tangier version of grilled amberjack—delicious!

Oriental Amberjack Steaks

2 lbs. amberjack steaks, thawed if frozen
¼ cup orange juice
1 cup soy sauce
2 tbsp. ketchup
2 tbsp. oil or butter
2 tbsp. chopped parsley
1 tbsp. lemon juice
½ tsp. oregano
½ tsp. pepper
1 clove garlic, minced

Place fish in a single layer in a shallow dish. Combine orange juice, soy sauce, ketchup, oil, parsley, lemon juice, oregano, pepper, and garlic. Pour marinade over fish and place in the refrigerator for 30 minutes, turning once. Remove fish and reserve marinade for basting. Place fish in a well-greased, hinged wire grill or in a well-greased 13 x 10-inch broiler pan. Cook over hot coals or under broiler approximately 4 inches from heat source for 4 to 5 minutes. Turn and baste with marinade. Cook 4 to 5 minutes more or until fish flakes easily with a fork. Serves 6.

Black Sea Bass

This small member of the sea bass family ranges from dark gray to almost blue-black in color and is usually recognized by its coloring and shape. They are not common in fresh markets but are sometimes caught by fishermen in both bays and the gulf, sometimes in remarkably large numbers. They are found primarily through the eastern half of the northern gulf and are rare west of Pensacola, Florida. The white, flaky flesh is quite good—so good, in fact, that it is caught commercially in some Atlantic-coast states.

Black Sea Bass Supreme

1 cup sour cream
1 tsp. celery salt
1 tsp. paprika
1 tsp. lemon juice
1 tsp. Worcestershire sauce
½ tsp. salt
¼ tsp. pepper
1 cup buttery cracker crumbs
½ cup walnuts, finely chopped
2 lbs. black sea bass fillets, skinned, thawed
    if frozen

Combine sour cream, celery salt, paprika, lemon juice, Worcestershire sauce, salt, and pepper. Chill 30 minutes to blend flavors. Preheat oven to 375 degrees. In a separate bowl, combine cracker crumbs and walnuts. Dip fish in sour cream mixture followed by crumb mixture. Place fish in a single layer on a well-greased 15 x 10-inch baking pan. Bake for 18 to 20 minutes or until fish flakes easily with a fork. Serves 6.

Sesame Grilled Black Sea Bass

2 lbs. black sea bass fillets, thawed if frozen
½ cup butter, melted
½ cup sesame seeds
¼ cup lemon juice
1 tsp. salt
⅛ tsp. pepper

Place black sea bass fillets in a well-greased, hinged wire grill. In a small bowl, combine butter, sesame seeds, lemon juice, salt, and pepper; baste fillets with mixture. Cook approximately 4 inches from moderately hot coals for 8 to 10 minutes. Turn fish and baste with sesame sauce. Cook 8 to 10 minutes longer or until fish flakes easily with a fork. Serves 6.

Microwave Fine Fish

½ to 1 stick of butter, melted
Juice of 1 lemon
1 to 2 tbsp. Sauterne wine
Tony Chachere's Creole Seasoning to taste
1 lb. fish fillets

Combine ingredients through Creole seasoning and pour over fish. Place fish, thick-side out, in a microwave-safe dish. Microwave 2½ minutes. Turn pan ½ turn. Microwave 2½ minutes more or until fish flakes easily with a fork. Serves 3 to 4.

Black Sea Bass Supreme

Just Delicious Fish

1 lb. fish fillets
Juice of 2 lemons
¾ cup mayonnaise
½ cup Parmesan cheese
Hot sauce to taste
½ stick of butter, melted

Bake or microwave fish until it flakes easily when tested with a fork. Mix remaining ingredients and spoon over fish. Broil until brown and puffy. Serves 3 to 4.

Blount County Fried Fish

1 lb. fish fillets
Cornmeal, enough to coat
Salt and pepper to taste

Soak fish fillets in ice water for 30 minutes to 1 hour. Remove fillets from water and place 3 or 4 in a bag with cornmeal, salt, and pepper. Shake to coat. Repeat with remaining fillets. Deep fry in hot peanut oil until golden brown. Serves 3 to 4.

Note: Blount County is a rural farming county in north central Alabama.

For a number of years, the Captain Duke *party boat plied the waters off Destin, Florida, for grouper, snapper, and other fish, including black sea bass. Earl Robinson owned and captained the boat. He so wanted his customers to enjoy their catch that he printed a free brochure with easy-to-prepare and delicious recipes. Captain Robinson passed away several years ago and the* Captain Duke *no longer operates. However, the Robinson heritage lives on through Earl's son, Scott Robinson, captain of the Destin charter boat* Stress Relief *that docks on the Destin Harbor. Just Delicious Fish, Blount County Fried Fish, and Microwave Fine Fish are included here under black sea bass because they work so well with that fish, but any other lean gulf fish will work equally well.*

Bluefish

Bluefish is a widely found sport fish, muscular and built for speed. It also is built with a mouthful of razor-sharp teeth to slay smaller fish, which compose its primary diet. Those teeth also will lacerate a careless fisherman's finger just as swiftly.

Silvery on the sides with a greenish-blue back, bluefish tend to grow to about five pounds in the gulf, a somewhat smaller average than the ten- to twenty-pound bruisers found along the Atlantic coast. Because they are pack hunters, when fishermen happen upon one bluefish, they typically load their cooler with many more. They are not common in markets but are caught frequently and easily, particularly in late fall.

The bluefish is a decent food fish, but it isn't considered to have the same level of quality as snapper and grouper.

Bluefish Salad Supreme

2 tbsp. vegetable oil
2 tbsp. red wine vinegar
2 tbsp. chopped onion
2 tbsp. green pepper
2 tbsp. chopped fresh parsley
¼ tsp. dried oregano
⅛ tsp. garlic powder
1 lb. skinless bluefish fillets, cooked and
  flaked
2 tbsp. sour cream
4 cups torn salad greens
2 medium tomatoes, cut into wedges

Combine oil, vinegar, onion, green pepper, parsley, oregano, and garlic powder in a large mixing bowl. Add fish and toss gently; chill thoroughly. Just before serving, stir in sour cream. Serve fish mixture on salad greens with tomato wedges. Serves 4.

Grilled Bluefish

¼ cup olive oil
¼ cup red wine vinegar
½ tsp. salt
½ tsp. pepper
1½ lbs. bluefish fillets

Combine the olive oil, vinegar, salt, and pepper in a shallow glass bowl. Put the bluefish in the bowl and let marinate several hours. Place fish on a well-greased grill over hot charcoal and baste liberally with marinade; turn over and baste every 4 to 5 minutes. Cook until fish flakes easily with a fork, about 10 minutes per inch of thickness. Serves 4.

Note: Grilling a bluefish tastes the same as almost any other grilled fish. Differing flavors in grilled fish typically comes from the marinade—in this case, wine, vinegar, salt, and pepper. However, many other flavor profiles will work as well. For a more citrus flavor, try a marinade of orange and lime juice with just a touch of dry white wine instead of the vinegar and oil. Adding a commercially manufactured citrus rub is a nice touch also.

Bluefish Salad Supreme

Grilled Bluefish with Fresh Corn Salsa

3 ears fresh or frozen corn, kernels removed
6 sprigs fresh cilantro, roughly chopped
2 tsp. finely diced red onion
1 jalapeño, seeded and finely chopped
Juice of 2 limes
1 pinch cumin
Salt and freshly ground black pepper to taste
4 6-8-oz. bluefish fillets
1 tsp. canola oil

In a non-corrosive bowl, combine corn, cilantro, ren onion, jalapeño, lime juice, cumin, salt, and pepper. Cover and let rest for at least 1 hour. Brush bluefish fillets with oil. Preheat oven to 225 degrees. On a medium-hot grill, cook bluefish for 2 to 3 minutes on each side. Remove from grill and place in oven for 3 to 5 minutes. While fillets are in the oven, heat a skillet until hot, add salsa, and cook for approximately 2 minutes or until all ingredients are warm. Remove from heat. Arrange bluefish on plates and garnish with salsa. Serves 4.

Festive Bluefish

½ lb. bluefish fillets
8 oz. Italian salad dressing
½ cup honey mustard pretzels, lightly crushed
Nonstick cooking spray

Preheat oven to 500 degrees. Remove and discard the skin and dark flesh from each fish fillet. Drizzle Italian dressing over fish, being sure to coat all sides. Roll fish in pretzel crumbs until thoroughly coated. Spray a pan with nonstick cooking spray and place fish in pan. Bake for about 10 to 12 minutes or until fish flakes easily with a fork. Serves 2.

Bluefish and Onions

2 lbs. bluefish fillets
Salt and pepper to taste
5 tbsp. olive oil, divided
2 cups coarsely chopped onion
1 tsp. minced garlic
2 tbsp. white vinegar

Preheat oven broiler to 500 degrees. Place fillets in a shallow dish. Sprinkle with salt, pepper, and 3 tbsp. olive oil. Let the fish sit while preparing other components. Sauté the onion in the remaining 2 tbsp. oil until wilted. Add garlic and additional salt and pepper to the onion and cook until soft. Drizzle vinegar over the onion and remove the pan from the heat. Broil bluefish for approximately 3 minutes. Turn fillets and cook for an additional 4 minutes or until fish flakes easily with a fork. Place fillets on plates and cover with cooked onions. Serves 6.

Gafftopsail Catfish

This is not the pesky hardhead catfish that fishermen consider a trash fish and avoid like the plague because of its sharp fins with which it enjoys impaling fishermen's hands. Nor is the gafftopsail catfish difficult to recognize from its ill-considered relative.

The gafftopsail is identified by the long, fleshy filaments extending from the first dorsal and pectoral spines. This is a fish most often brought home by fishermen than found in a fresh market. While its flesh is darker than most lean fish, the flesh doesn't have the strong taste of a mackerel and is considered good table fare.

They are cleaned and prepared like any other catfish.

Old-Fashioned Buttermilk Catfish

Old-Fashioned Buttermilk Catfish

1 lb. catfish fillets
1 cup buttermilk
Salt and pepper to taste
½ cup cornmeal, plus additional if needed
½ cup flour, plus additional if needed
Vegetable oil, for frying

Cut fish fillets into strips approximately 1-inch wide. Combine the buttermilk, salt, and pepper in a bowl. Place the fish in the buttermilk mixture, taking care to see that each fillet is fully covered. Place the bowl in the refrigerator at least 2 hours. Preheat enough oil to cover the fish in a deep fryer to 375 degrees. Combine flour and cornmeal in a shallow bowl or on a piece of waxed paper. Take the fish out of the buttermilk mixture, dredge in the cornmeal mixture, and place them in the oil. Fry until golden brown. Serves 3 to 4.

Note: Rare is the rural-raised Southerner who did not experience a regular serving of this dish. It is a classic recipe for every fish that grows whiskers.

Fast Catfish Broil

2 lbs. skinless gafftopsail catfish fillets, thawed if frozen
¼ cup garlic French dressing
3 tbsp. soy sauce
¾ tsp. ground ginger
Lime slices, for garnish

Place catfish fillets in a single layer, skinned side down, on a 16 x 10-inch ovenproof platter. Combine French dressing, soy sauce, and ginger. Pour sauce over fillets and let stand for 10 minutes. Broil about 4 inches from heat source for 10 to 15 minutes or until fish flakes easily with a fork, basting once with additional sauce. Garnish with lime slices. Serves 6.

Note: If you can't find garlic French dressing, substitute with French dressing and ¼ tsp. garlic powder.

Gafftopsail Catfish in Cream

1½ lbs. gafftopsail catfish fillets
1 tbsp. grated onion
½ tsp. dried dill
Dash salt
3 tbsp. butter
½ cup light cream

Preheat oven to 350 degrees. Place fish in a greased baking dish. Sprinkle with onion, dill, and salt. Dot with butter. Pour cream over fillets. Bake for about 20 minutes or until fish flakes easily with a fork. Serves 4.

Greek Catfish

2 tbsp. olive oil
¼ cup chopped lemon, peeled and sectioned
1 tbsp. minced green onion
1 tbsp. chopped black olives
1 tbsp. chopped parsley
¼ tsp. oregano
1 small garlic clove, minced
1¼ lbs. catfish fillets

Combine olive oil, lemon, green onion, olives, parsley, oregano, and garlic in a bowl. Coat a broiler pan with cooking oil, and place the catfish in the pan. Pour the olive oil mixture evenly over the catfish, reserving some for serving. Broil approximately 4 inches from the heat for 6 to 8 minutes. Place fish on platter and pour remaining olive oil mixture ingredients over fish. Serves 3 to 4.

Note: Feel free to substitute thyme for the oregano.

If fish looks dry during broiling, baste with some of the reserved olive oil mixture.

Heavenly Catfish

2 lbs. skinless gafftopsail catfish, thawed if frozen
2 tbsp. lemon juice
½ cup grated Parmesan cheese
¼ cup butter, softened
3 tbsp. mayonnaise or salad dressing
3 tbsp. chopped green onion
¼ tsp. salt
⅛ tsp. liquid hot sauce

Place fish fillets in a single layer on a well-greased 16 x 10-inch ovenproof platter. Brush fillets with lemon juice and let stand for 10 minutes. Combine Parmesan cheese, butter, mayonnaise, green onion, salt, and hot sauce, and set aside. Broil fillets about 4 inches from heat source for 6 to 8 minutes or until fish flakes easily with a fork. Cover fish with cheese mixture. Broil 2 to 3 minutes more or until lightly browned. Serves 6.

Cobia

This long, dark brown fish is easily identifiable by the silvery white streaks down its side and a deeply forked tail—not to mention its size. These are big fish, commonly between 20 and 40 pounds and occasionally 100 pounds. Each spring, they migrate in small groups from east to west along the coast, often following the outermost sandbar, and then settle over wrecks and reefs during the warm summer months. In the winter, they migrate back to warmer, tropical waters.

Fishermen aggressively seek these fish in the spring by slowly cruising just outside the outer sandbar and looking for them from the boat's tuna tower high above the water. When fishermen spot the cobia, they cast brightly colored artificial lures, live baitfish, or, most often, a live eel where the cobia can see it. Eel seems to be a favorite cobia snack. The eels are usually of the fresh-water variety and live only a short time in salt water—a *really* short time if a cobia takes an interest.

Cobia—also called ling and lemonfish—are considered excellent food fish and can be found in local markets in season. When preparing a cobia for cooking, be sure to cut out the dark red flesh that runs down each side.

Cobia in Wine Sauce

6 cobia fillets
½ cup flour
Salt and pepper to taste
2 tbsp. minced garlic
1 large white onion, chopped
1 bunch green onions, chopped
1 cup butter
1½ cups white wine
Juice of 2 lemons
Parsley, chopped, for garnish

Coat cobia fillets in flour seasoned with salt and pepper. Pan-fry fillets until lightly brown. Set aside on paper towels to drain excess oil. In a separate pan, sauté garlic, white onion, and green onions in butter until tender. Add wine and stir for 3 minutes. Remove from heat and add fish fillets to sauce. Let simmer until all fillets are cooked. Sprinkle with lemon before juice serving and garnish with fresh parsley. Serves 6.

Lime-Grilled Cobia

Cobia steaks, enough for each person
Salt and pepper to taste
Old Bay seasoning to taste
Garlic power to taste
Lime vinaigrette
Fresh lime juice, usually 1 lime per 4 steaks.

Season cobia with salt, pepper, Old Bay seasoning, and garlic power. Place in a dish and pour enough lime vinaigrette over steaks to cover. Marinate in the refrigerator for 1 hour. Grill approximately 4 inches from heat for 5 to 6 minutes. Turn carefully and grill an additional 5 to 6 minutes or until fish flakes easily with a fork. Squeeze lime juice over steaks and serve.

Note: This recipe can feed as large or as small a group as you like, so simply adjust the quantities for the size of the party! One bottle of lime vinaigrette is almost assuredly enough to marinate all of the steaks that would fit on a grill at one time.

If you are prone to breaking fillets and having them fall through the grill onto the coals when turning them, a hinged, wire fish basket is an excellent tool to keep that from happening.

Feel free to substitute other citrus vinaigrettes or dressings in place of the lime vinaigrette.

Greek Cobia Fillets

4 cobia fillets
½ cup flour
½ cup olive oil
1 cup chopped onion
1 clove garlic, minced
1 28-oz. can chopped tomatoes
¼ cup black olives, chopped
1 tbsp. capers, drained
½ tsp. sweet basil
½ tsp. salt
¼ tsp. pepper
Garlic-flavored croutons, for garnish

Coat cobia fillets in flour. Fry in olive oil over moderate heat for 4 to 5 minutes or until brown. Turn and cook 4 to 5 minutes more or until fish flakes easily with a fork. Place on a serving dish and keep warm. In the same oil, fry onion and garlic until tender. Add tomatoes, olives, capers, basil, salt, and pepper. Cook for 5 minutes. Spoon over fish and serve with croutons. Serves 4.

Grilled Cobia Steaks

¼ cup French dressing
1 tbsp. lemon juice
1 tbsp. grated onion
1 tsp. salt
¼ tsp. pepper
2 lbs. cobia steaks, thawed if frozen

Combine French dressing, lemon juice, onion, salt, and pepper; mix well. Baste steaks with sauce. Place fish in a well-greased, hinged wire grill. Cook about 4 inches from hot coals for 8 minutes. Baste with sauce. Turn and cook for an additional 7 to 10 minutes or until fish flakes easily with a fork. Serves 6.

Herb-Seasoned Cobia Steaks

1 tsp. salt
¼ tsp. white pepper
2 lbs. cobia steaks
Juice of 1 lime
½ cup chopped green onion
½ tsp. thyme
1 tsp. chopped garlic
2 tomatoes, sliced

Preheat oven to 375 degrees. Sprinkle salt and pepper on all sides of cobia steaks. Place in a lightly greased, shallow baking dish. Pour lime juice over steaks and sprinkle with green onion, thyme, and garlic. Top with tomato slices. Bake for 20 to 25 minutes or until fish flakes easily with a fork. Serves 6.

Greek Cobia Fillets

Croaker

The casual observer could easily mistake the Atlantic croaker for its croaking cousins, the Southern kingfish, also known as ground mullet, and the exceedingly tasty gulf kingfish, also known as whiting, because they all have a similar color and shape.

More specifically, the croaker is a tasty panfish, sought commercially for shipment to foreign markets, where it is prized. The easy way to separate the Atlantic croaker from its cousins is to check its chin to see if the six to ten tiny fleshy "whiskers" are present. They are much smaller than the big whiskers of the black drum.

The Atlantic croaker is white and has faint vertical bars along each side. It is common in both fresh markets and in the coolers of fishermen who seek them in bays, inlets, jetties, and lakes and rivers near the gulf. They commonly reach one foot in length and weigh about one pound, although an offshore fisherman occasionally is surprised by a four- or five-pounder. The larger ones tend to be found well offshore.

Chipper Croaker

2 lbs. croaker fillets, thawed if frozen
½ cup Caesar salad dressing
1 cup potato chips, crushed
½ cup shredded sharp cheddar cheese

Preheat oven to 500 degrees. Dip croaker fillets in salad dressing. Place fillets in a single layer, skin-side down, on a 15 x 10-inch lightly greased baking pan. Combine crushed chips and cheese; sprinkle over fillets. Bake for 10 to 15 minutes or until fillets flake easily with a fork. Serves 6.

Croaker Stir-Fry

1 lb. skinless croaker fillets
½ cup white wine
1 tbsp. sesame oil
2 cloves garlic, minced
1 tsp. minced fresh ginger
½ tsp. onion powder
¼ tsp. pepper
1 tbsp. vegetable oil
2 cups fresh mushrooms, sliced
½ cup chopped celery
½ cup chopped green onion
1 cup broccoli florets
4 servings rice, cooked according to package directions

Cut fish into 1-inch cubes. Combine wine, sesame oil, garlic, ginger, onion powder, and pepper in a large bowl. Add fish, cover, and refrigerate for 30 minutes. Heat vegetable oil in a wok or frying pan. Stir-fry mushrooms, celery, green onion, and broccoli until barely tender. Add fish and marinade to vegetables and stir-fry over medium heat for 4 to 6 minutes or until fish flakes easily with a fork. Serve over rice. Serves 4.

Western-Style Croaker

2 lbs. croaker fillets, thawed if frozen
1 tsp. salt
¼ tsp. pepper
¼ tsp. paprika
1½ cups chopped tomatoes
⅔ cup chopped parsley
½ cup pimiento-stuffed olives, sliced
⅓ cup diced lemon, peeled and sectioned

Preheat oven to 400 degrees. Sprinkle croaker with salt, pepper, and paprika. Place fish in a shallow 12 x 8-inch baking dish. Combine tomatoes, parsley, olives, and lemon, and spread over the top of the fish. Cover with foil and bake for 10 minutes. Uncover; continue to bake for 18 to 20 minutes or until fish flakes easily with a fork. Serves 6.

Herbed Croaker 'n Chips

½ cup mayonnaise
¼ cup chopped chives
¼ cup chopped parsley
1½ tbsp. lemon juice
1 tsp. grated lemon zest
¼ tsp. kosher salt
Dash hot sauce
1¼ lbs. croaker fillets
1 6-oz. bag potato chips, for serving

In a small mixing bowl, whisk together mayonnaise, chives, parsley, lemon juice, lemon zest, salt, and hot sauce. Transfer half of the mixture into a separate bowl; cover, refrigerate, and set aside. Heat a large, nonstick pan or griddle over medium-high heat. Brush croaker fillets with remaining herb mayonnaise. Place each fillet, coated side down, onto the preheated pan, and cook for 2 to 3 minutes until golden. Using a spatula, turn and brown the remaining side for another 1 to 2 minutes until cooked through. Transfer cooked fillets onto a serving plate, and top each portion with approximately 1½ tbsp. of reserved herb mayonnaise. Serve with potato chips on the side. Serves 4.

Quick Croaker

2 cups chopped onion
¼ cup oil
2 lbs. skinless croaker fillets, thawed if frozen
1½ tsp. salt
¼ tsp. pepper
2 tomatoes, sliced
1 lemon, sliced
1 large bay leaf
¼ cup water
1 tsp. sugar
1 tsp. cider vinegar
French bread, for serving

Cook onion in oil in a 10-inch fry pan until tender. While onion is cooking, cut croaker fillets cross-wise into strips about ½-inch wide. Arrange fish over onion. Sprinkle with salt and pepper. Cover croaker with tomato and lemon slices. Add bay leaf. In a small bowl, combine water, sugar, and vinegar. Pour over fish mixture. Cover and simmer for 10 to 15 minutes or until fish flakes easily with a fork. Serve with French bread. Serves 6.

Quick Croaker

Cusk Eel

This is an ugly fish. Also known as gulf cod, it is a cousin of the cod and has a mild flavor, not unlike grouper. Fishermen working deep water for grouper are usually the ones who bring up this odd catch. Only on rare occasions can this creature be found in fresh markets.

Despite its tastiness, there are few recipes unique to the cusk eel. Use recipes for grouper to prepare this fish.

Dolphin, Also Known As Mahi-Mahi

This is the dolphin fish, not the mammal (think *Flipper)* that many call a dolphin but is actually a porpoise. Also called mahi-mahi, the dolphin is one of the northern gulf's tastiest and most beautiful fish. It also is a fisherman's delight because of its fighting abilities and its propensity to leap high in the air in an attempt to throw the hook.

Dolphin can be found far offshore in the same waters where northern gulf fishermen search for marlin as well as near shore in mats of seaweed and other floating objects. They are prolific in both breeding and growth, so there always seems to be plenty to catch. The near-shore fish tend to range from one to three feet, while larger fish—up to six feet long—are most often found farther offshore.

They are an excellent food fish, with grilling one of the preferred cooking methods. When grilling, leave the skin on the fillet to prevent the delicate meat from falling through the grill.

Broiled Dolphin with Tangy Glaze

2 lbs. skinless dolphin fillets
⅓ cup vegetable oil
⅓ cup ketchup
⅓ cup frozen lemonade concentrate, thawed
1 tbsp. prepared mustard
½ tsp. salt
½ tsp. garlic salt
1 large bay leaf, crumbled

Cut fish into serving-size portions and arrange in a single layer in a baking dish. Combine vegetable oil, ketchup, lemonade concentrate, mustard, salt, garlic salt, and bay leaf; mix well. Pour marinade over fillets, being sure to coat evenly. Cover and marinate in refrigerator for 30 minutes. Place fish on a lightly greased broiler pan. Baste with marinade; broil 4 inches from heat for 4 to 5 minutes on each side, basting with additional marinade when turning fish. Cook until fish flakes easily with a fork. Serves 6.

Grilled Mahi-Mahi with Lime

4 6-oz. mahi-mahi fillets
Juice of 2 key limes
Zest of 2 key limes
3 tbsp. extra virgin olive oil
2 tbsp. dry white wine
1 tsp. fresh rosemary
½ tsp. fresh thyme
¼ tsp. black pepper, coarsely ground
Fresh herbs, for garnish
Lime slices, for garnish

Place the mahi-mahi fillets in a shallow dish. Combine the lime juice, lime zest, olive oil, white wine, rosemary, thyme, and black pepper in a small bowl; mix well. Pour the marinade over the fish and marinate for 1 hour in refrigerator. Preheat a greased grill on medium-high heat. Grill fillets for 4 to 5 minutes on each side until center is opaque and meat flakes easily with a fork. Garnish with herbs and lime slices. Serves 4.

Sesame Dolphin Bites

1 lb. skinless dolphin fillets
⅓ cup white wine
3 tbsp. mango chutney
3 tbsp. vegetable oil
1 tsp. curry powder
½ tsp. salt
¼ cup sesame seeds

Cut dolphin fillets into 1-inch cubes. In a small bowl, combine wine, chutney, vegetable oil, curry powder, and salt. Pour over fish, being sure to coat thoroughly. Cover and marinate for 1 hour in the refrigerator, stirring once. Remove fish from marinade and sprinkle all sides with sesame seeds. Place in a lightly-oiled baking dish and broil 5 to 6 inches from heat for 5 to 7 minutes or until fish flakes easily with a fork. Serves 3 to 4.

Pan-Seared Mahi-Mahi Tacos with Guacamole and Pico de Gallo

1 small head red cabbage, shredded
2 tbsp. vegetable oil
3 tbsp. fresh lime juice
Salt and pepper to taste
2 tbsp. butter
1 tbsp. extra virgin olive oil
2 lbs. skinless mahi-mahi fillets
10 7-inch tortillas, warmed
Fresh guacamole (recipe below), for serving
Fresh Pico de Gallo (recipe below), for serving
Lime wedges, for serving

Guacamole

2 avocados, halved, pitted, and peeled
Juice of 1 lime
2 tbsp. minced red onion
2 tbsp. fresh cilantro, chopped, plus more for
   garnish
1 tomato, diced
Salt and pepper to taste

Pico de Gallo

1 large tomato, diced
½ cup red onion, finely diced
⅓ cup fresh cilantro, chopped
Fresh lime juice to taste

In a large bowl, toss the cabbage with the vegetable oil and lime juice. Season with salt and pepper. Set aside. Add the butter and olive oil to a large skillet and melt over medium heat. Season the mahi-mahi fillets with salt and pepper; place into the skillet. Cook for approximately 4 to 5 minutes per side or until the fish is cooked through. Remove the fillets to a cutting board and slice into strips. To assemble the tacos, spread about 2 tbsp. of the guacamole on half of a warmed tortilla. Top with several strips of mahi-mahi, followed by a large spoonful of the cabbage slaw. Finish it off with a sprinkling of Pico de Gallo. Serve with lime wedges. Serves 4.

In a medium bowl, mash the avocados with a fork. Add the lime juice, red onion, cilantro, and tomato. Stir well. Season with salt and pepper to taste. Press a piece of plastic wrap directly onto the surface of the guacamole until ready to use to prevent it from changing color. Garnish with additional cilantro.

Combine tomato, red onion, cilantro, and lime juice in a small bowl. Stir well and refrigerate until cold.

Note: "These Pan-Seared Mahi-Mahi Tacos are scrumptious! They are beautiful when plated and have an incredibly fresh and citrusy flavor. The creamy guacamole, when paired with the fresh lime and cilantro in the Pico de Gallo, results in one stellar combination," says photographer and food writer Celeste Ward, who developed the dish.

Pan-Seared Mahi-Mahi Tacos with
Guacamole and Pico de Gallo

Mahi-Mahi à la Pepper

1½ lbs. skinless mahi-mahi fillets
1 tsp. garlic salt
½ tsp. lemon pepper
2 tbsp. vegetable oil
½ tsp. instant chicken bouillon
¼ cup tomato sauce
1 tsp. capers
½ medium green pepper, cut in rings
½ medium red bell pepper, cut in rings

Cut mahi-mahi into 4-inch pieces. Sprinkle fish with garlic salt and lemon pepper. In a 12-inch skillet, cook fish in oil over moderate heat for 5 minutes, turning often. Dissolve bouillon in ½ cup boiling water. Add chicken broth, tomato sauce, and capers to fish; reduce heat, cover, and simmer for 10 minutes. Top with pepper rings and cook, uncovered, for 5 minutes or until peppers are tender and fish flakes easily with a fork. Serves 4.

Mahi-Mahi Pontchartrain

2 lbs. skinned mahi-mahi fillets, thawed if
    frozen
¼ cup butter, melted
8 oz. raw shrimp, peeled, deveined, and
    chopped, thawed if frozen
¼ cup chopped green onion
½ cup fresh mushrooms, sliced
½ cup dry white wine
2 tbsp. Worcestershire sauce
1 tbsp. lemon juice
½ tsp. salt
¼ tsp. thyme

Cut mahi-mahi into serving-size portions. In a large skillet, cook fish in butter for 2 minutes on each side. In a large bowl, combine shrimp, green onion, mushrooms, white wine, Worcestershire sauce, lemon juice, salt, and thyme; pour over fish. Cover and cook over low heat for 8 to 10 minutes or until fish flakes easily with a fork. Serves 6.

Drum, Red and Black

The drum family is a big one that includes seatrout, croaker, whiting, black drum, and red drum, also known as redfish. The name comes from the noisy vibration that they produce. The black drum is a dark grayish brown with several dark bars running from the back to the belly. These fish are bottom feeders, tending to gather in deep holes and channels. They grow to seventy pounds or more, but when they get that big, they are so hard to clean that most fishermen don't bother. On the other hand, the smaller one- to two-pound drum can be substituted for redfish.

In the drum family, the red drum—or redfish, as it is frequently known—is by far the tonier species. Made famous by the New Orleans dish of Blackened Redfish, the fish's population rapidly shrank as every restaurant felt it had to offer their own variation. Regulators placed stringent length and creel limitations on redfish in 1987, when it was given gamefish status, which prevented it from being harvested commercially. The population has recovered nicely. Still, these coppery-colored fish carry limits to prevent a return to overfishing. Redfish are found in both near-shore gulf and bay waters and often are seen in schools, with individual fish averaging thirty or forty pounds. They are tough fighters on the hook and line and are a frequently sought target of fall and winter fishermen in the northern gulf.

When cleaning, fishermen often cut from just behind the gills upward to the spine in order to sever a major blood vessel and allow the fish to drain for several minutes before completing the butchering. They believe that this improves the flavor of the flesh.

Broiled Drum

4 8-oz. boneless redfish or black drum fillets
½ cup butter, melted
1 tbsp. lemon pepper
½ tsp. cayenne pepper
1 large onion, thinly sliced, separated into
    rings
2 tsp. Worcestershire sauce
2 lemons

Preheat oven to 450 degrees. Coat fish fillets in melted butter and place on a nonstick broiler pan. Sprinkle fish evenly with lemon pepper and cayenne pepper. Place onion rings on the fillets and then drizzle with Worcestershire sauce. Bake for 8 minutes on the center oven rack, then raise the heat to a 500-degree broil, move fish to the top rack, and cook long enough to brown the fish and onions, approximately 3 to 6 minutes, being careful not to overcook. Remove and allow to cool for 3 minutes. Squeeze lemons over fish and serve. Serves 4.

Ginger-Honey Drum

1½ lbs. drum fillets
1 cup honey
2 tsp. ground ginger
1 red bell pepper, seeded, cut into 2-inch
    strips
1 yellow bell pepper, seeded, cut into 2-inch
    strips

Cut fillets into serving-size pieces; set aside. Combine honey and ginger; use half of honey mixture to coat fish evenly. Place fish on an oiled grill over medium-hot coals; baste frequently with honey mixture and turn once during cooking. Coat bell peppers with remaining honey mixture and grill until tender, turning often to avoid burning. Fish is done when it flakes easily with a fork, approximately 10 minutes per inch of thickness. Serves 4.

Grilled Redfish

¾ cup mayonnaise
1 tsp. steak sauce
1 tsp. lime juice
2 tbsp. grated Parmesan cheese
⅛ tsp. fresh dill, minced
4 redfish fillets

Mix mayonnaise, steak sauce, lime juice, cheese, and dill. Spread generously on both sides of fillets. Place coated fillets on grill and cook for 3 to 5 minutes per side or until fish flakes easily with a fork. Serves 4.

Oven-Fried Redfish

1½ lbs. redfish fillets
Vegetable oil, enough to coat fillets
Salt and pepper to taste
1 cup Italian bread crumbs, plus additional as needed
2 sticks butter, melted, divided
Juice of 1 lemon
Dash of Worcestershire sauce

Preheat oven to 400 degrees. Pat fish dry and coat thoroughly with vegetable oil. Season with salt and pepper and roll in bread crumbs. Coat a baking pan with 1 stick melted butter; place fish in pan, skin-side down. Bake, uncovered, for 20 to 25 minutes or until golden brown. Do not turn. In a small bowl, combine remaining 1 stick melted butter, lemon juice, and Worcestershire sauce. Use sauce to baste; serve with meal. Serves 4 to 6.

Blackened Redfish

2 tsp. ground thyme
2 tsp. ground marjoram
2 tsp. garlic powder
1 tsp. ground oregano
1 tsp. cayenne pepper
1 tsp. paprika
1 tsp. salt
1 tsp. white pepper
1½ lbs. redfish fillets, thawed if frozen
Butter, enough to coat all fish fillets

Combine thyme, marjoram, garlic powder, ground oregano, cayenne pepper, paprika, salt, and white pepper. Heat a large, lightly oiled cast-iron skillet over high heat until a drop of water sizzles in pan, about 10 minutes. Coat both sides of the fish fillets with butter. Sprinkle fish with spice mixture, shaking off any excess. Place fillets in the hot skillet and cook 2 to 3 minutes per side or until fish flakes easily with a fork. Serves 4 to 6.

Note: This dish, created in New Orleans, led to the initial decimation of the redfish population. As a result of its popularity, regulators instituted size and creel limits in order to rebuild the stock. Redfish are again in good supply, and populations all along the northern gulf coast appear to be thriving.

Great Gulf Redfish Chowder

1 lb. redfish fillets, thawed if frozen
1½ cups water, divided
½ tsp. salt
1 10-oz. package frozen baby lima beans
½ tsp. seasoned salt
2 10¾-oz. cans condensed cream of chicken soup
1½ cups milk
2 tsp. onion powder
⅛ tsp. hot sauce
1 tsp. chopped fresh parsley, for garnish

Cut fish into 1-inch pieces. Combine fish, ½ cup water, and salt in a small saucepan. Cover and bring to a boil. Set aside. Combine remaining 1 cup water, lima beans, and seasoned salt in a 3-quart saucepan; bring to a boil. Cover and simmer for 10 minutes or until beans are tender. Add condensed soup, milk, onion powder, and hot sauce; stir well to combine. Add fish and saltwater to soup mixture. Cover and bring to a simmer; simmer for 10 minutes. Garnish with chopped parsley and serve. Serves 6.

Blackened Redfish

Italian-Style Redfish

2 lbs. redfish fillets, skinned, thawed if frozen
1½ cups chopped celery
½ cup chopped onion
1 clove garlic, minced
¼ cup butter
1 12-oz. can tomatoes, undrained
1 8-oz. can tomato sauce
2 tsp. salt
¼ tsp. pepper
½ tsp. chili powder
½ tsp. oregano leaves
1 7-oz. package uncooked spaghetti
2 cups boiling water
¼ cup grated Parmesan cheese, for garnish
Hot garlic bread, for serving

Cut redfish fillets into 1-inch cubes. In a 6-quart saucepan, cook celery, onion, and garlic in butter until tender. Add tomatoes, tomato sauce, salt, pepper, chili powder, and oregano. Cover and simmer for 5 to 10 minutes. Add spaghetti and water. Mix well. Cover and simmer for 10 minutes or until spaghetti is almost tender. Add fish and continue to cook for 8 to 10 minutes or until fish flakes easily with a fork. Garnish with Parmesan cheese. Serve with hot garlic bread. Serves 6.

Savory Baked Drum

2 lbs. drum fillets, thawed if frozen
2 tsp. lemon juice
½ tsp. salt
⅛ tsp. pepper
6 slices bacon, diced
½ cup onion, sliced into rings
½ cup soft bread crumbs
2 tbsp. chopped parsley
Pimiento strips, for garnish

Preheat oven to 350 degrees. Cut fish into serving-size portions. Place fish in a well-greased 12 x 8-inch baking dish. Sprinkle with lemon juice, salt and pepper. In a small pan, fry bacon until crisp. Drain pieces on absorbent paper; reserve the drippings. Cook onion in bacon drippings until tender, and arrange evenly over fish fillets. Combine bacon, bread crumbs, and parsley. Sprinkle mixture over fish. Bake for 20 minutes or until fish flakes easily with a fork. Garnish with pimiento strips. Serves 6.

Flounder

There is no mistaking the flounder, no matter the species. They all have one white side and one mottled brown side. Both of their eyes are on the brown side of their heads. These flatfish lay on their sides on the bottom of the gulf, white side down, blending in with their surroundings until they explode from hiding to capture a careless or unsuspecting minnow for an easy meal. Their delicate, white, and tasty flesh makes them a favorite for fishermen and fresh markets alike. Keepers average from just more than one foot in length to more than three feet and weighing more than ten pounds.

Flounder are found in both the open gulf and bays, although they tend to migrate out of the bays and onto close-to-shore reefs when the water cools in the fall. They settle around those reefs for the winter, then return to the bays when the water warms. Fishing action—particularly in channels leading from the bay to the gulf—is often busy in the fall when the flounder migrate to open water.

They are a fresh-market favorite and usually are available year around.

Flash-in-the-Pan Flounder

4 6-oz. flounder fillets
1 tsp. salt, divided
1 tbsp. flour
2 tbsp. vegetable oil
1 10-oz. bag frozen yellow corn
3 tbsp. lemon juice
1 10-oz. bag baby spinach
½ pt. small cherry tomatoes, rinsed

Season flounder with ½ tsp. salt and dust with flour. Heat oil in a large nonstick sauté pan over high heat. Add flounder and cook for 2 to 3 minutes until lightly browned; turn and cook on other side for 1 to 2 minutes. Transfer to a clean baking sheet and set aside in a warm oven. Stir yellow corn, lemon juice, and remaining ½ tsp. salt into pan and cook for 1 to 2 minutes. Add spinach; continue cooking and stirring for 2 minutes until spinach has just wilted and corn is heated through, then toss in cherry tomatoes. Divide evenly onto 4 plates and top with flounder. Serves 4.

Flounder Amandine

1 lb. skinless flounder fillets
2 tbsp. butter, melted
1 tbsp. lemon juice
⅛ tsp. pepper
⅛ tsp. onion powder
⅛ tsp. nutmeg
1 tbsp. slivered, blanched almonds
Chopped fresh parsley, for garnish

Place flounder fillets in a shallow baking pan that has been coated with nonstick cooking spray. In a small bowl, combine butter, lemon juice, pepper, onion powder, and nutmeg. Brush most of it on the fish. Broil 4 to 6 inches from heat for 4 to 6 minutes or until fish flakes easily with a fork. During the last few minutes of cooking, moisten almonds with remaining sauce and spread over fish to lightly brown. Sprinkle with parsley before serving. Serves 4.

Flounder with Citrus Marinade

Juice of 2 limes
Juice of 1 orange (or ¼ cup orange juice
    concentrate)
2 sprigs fresh rosemary (or 1 tbsp. dried
    rosemary)
4 flounder fillets

In a shallow dish, combine lime juice, orange juice, and rosemary. Add fish. Cover with plastic wrap and refrigerate for 1 hour. Remove fish from refrigerator, spray with cooking oil, and grill for 4 to 5 minutes per side. Serves 4.

Note: Alternatively, bake the fish in a 375-degree oven for 30 minutes.

Crab-Stuffed Flounder

6 ¾-lb. pan-dressed flounders, thawed if
    frozen
1 recipe Blue Crab Stuffing
2 tsp. salt
¾ cup butter, melted
⅓ cup lemon juice
2 tbsp. water
2 tsp. salt
Paprika to taste

Preheat oven to 350 degrees. Place flounder, light side down, on a work surface. With a sharp knife, cut lengthwise down the center of the dark side of the fish, approximately 1 inch from the gills to 1 inch from the tail. Tilt the knife sideways to cut horizontally along the backbone on each side of the cut to form a pocket in which to place the stuffing. Stuff fish loosely, approximately ⅔ cup stuffing per fish. Place fish in 2 well-greased 16 x 11-inch baking dishes. In a small dish, combine butter, lemon juice, water, and salt. Pour butter mixture over the fish. Sprinkle with paprika. Bake for 25 to 30 minutes or until fish flakes easily when tested with a fork. Serves 6.

Flounder Mushroom Medley

2 cups fresh mushrooms, sliced
½ cup chopped green pepper
1 clove garlic, minced
3 tbsp. butter, melted
½ cup dry white wine
1½ lbs. skinless, boneless flounder fillets,
    thawed if frozen
2 tbsp. chopped pimiento
½ tsp. salt
¼ tsp. white pepper
¼ tsp. Italian or Greek herb blend
Chopped fresh parsley, for garnish

In a large skillet over medium heat, cook mushrooms, green pepper, and garlic in butter for 5 minutes, stirring occasionally. Stir in wine and bring to a boil. Add fish to pan. Sprinkle pimiento, salt, pepper, and herb blend over fillets. Cover, reduce heat, and simmer for 20 to 25 minutes or until fish flakes easily with a fork. Garnish with parsley. Serves 4.

Flounder Casserole

1 cup chopped celery
¼ cup butter, melted
2 cups cooked, flaked flounder
1 10¾-oz. can condensed cream of
    mushroom soup
1 cup cracker crumbs
3 hard-boiled eggs, chopped
¾ cup shredded Cheddar cheese, divided
Paprika to taste

Preheat oven to 375 degrees. In a 10-inch skillet, cook celery in butter until tender. Add fish, soup, cracker crumbs, eggs, and ¼ cup cheese; mix well. Place fish mixture in a well-greased 1½-quart casserole dish. Sprinkle with ½ cup cheese and paprika. Bake for 20 to 25 minutes or until heated through and cheese is melted. Serves 6.

Flounder Mushroom Medley

Grouper

If one universal characteristic could be named about groupers, perhaps it would be that they have large mouths. Besides this feature, they come in a variety of colors, sizes, and even shapes—some are stocky and short, others are long.

Fishermen often catch groupers of less than one pound in the bay and of anywhere ten to sixty pounds in the gulf. A couple of them—the Warsaw and the goliath—grow to more than six feet in length and weigh more than five hundred pounds.

Grouper can be found in bays and out in the gulf near deep offshore reefs. Probably most common in the northern gulf are the gag, scamp, and red groupers, with a number of others following close behind.

An interesting tidbit is that groupers develop as females. As they reach maturity, they can become male as the need arises.

Fishermen target this species, and fresh markets seem to always have fresh grouper steaks and fillets. All are excellent for almost any type of cooking, with the scamp tending to be the most prized.

Chorizo- and Crab-Stuffed Grouper

6 tbsp. butter, divided
1 lb. chorizo sausage
½ medium red onion, finely chopped
1 rib celery, finely chopped
½ medium red bell pepper, finely chopped
5 cloves garlic, finely chopped
4 green onions, finely sliced
1 tbsp. dried oregano
1½ tbsp. ground cumin, plus additional to taste
¼ cup tequila
¼ cup chicken stock
¼ cup heavy cream
½ lb. crab meat
¼ cup mayonnaise
1½ cups Panko bread crumbs
8 6-oz. grouper fillets

Melt 3 tbsp. butter in a sauté pan. Crumble chorizo into butter and cook through. Add red onion, celery, bell pepper, garlic, green onions, oregano, and cumin; cook for 3 minutes over medium-high heat. Remove from heat and pour in tequila; return to high heat and reduce by half. Add chicken stock and cream; reduce by half. Remove from heat and let cool. Gently incorporate crab meat, mayonnaise, and bread crumbs to chorizo mixture, being careful to not break up the crab meat, then place in the refrigerator. Lay grouper fillets on a cutting board and butterfly, being careful not to cut all the way through. Make a ball of stuffing. Press onto one side of the fish into a layer about ½-inch thick. Fold fillet over to cover stuffing. Repeat with remaining fillets; keep in refrigerator until ready to cook. Preheat oven to 350 degrees. Dust each fillet with cumin to taste. Melt remaining 3 tbsp. butter over medium-high heat, and sauté each fillet on the top until golden brown. Transfer to a buttered baking sheet and bake in the oven for 5 minutes or until fish flakes easily with a fork. Serves 8.

Grayton Beach Grouper Soup

1½ lbs. grouper fillets
1 tsp. paprika
2 15-oz. cans tomato sauce
8 oz. fresh mushrooms, sliced
1 tsp. thyme
1 tsp. marjoram
1 tsp. savory
1 cup chopped green onions

Cut grouper fillets into approximately 2-inch cubes; sprinkle with paprika. Lightly grease a large skillet with nonstick cooking spray. Brown fish over medium-high heat until it flakes easily. Remove fish from skillet, set aside, and keep warm. In the same skillet, combine tomato sauce, mushrooms, thyme, marjoram, and savory and simmer on medium-low heat until mushrooms are tender. Divide tomato sauce mixture evenly into four soup bowls; add fish and top with green onions. Serves 4.

Buttery Baked Grouper

4 tbsp. butter, melted, divided
2 tbsp. fresh lemon juice, divided
4 6-oz. grouper fillets
Salt and pepper to taste
3 tbsp. mayonnaise
½ cup saltine cracker crumbs
⅓ cup slivered almonds, toasted
Lemon wedges, for garnish

Preheat oven to 400 degrees. Combine 1 tbsp. melted butter with 1 tbsp. lemon juice in a 13 x 9-inch baking dish. Arrange fillets in dish; sprinkle with salt and pepper. Spread mayonnaise evenly over the top of the fillets. In a small bowl, combine cracker crumbs, the remaining 3 tbsp. melted butter, almonds, and remaining 1 tbsp. lemon juice; sprinkle over fillets. Bake, uncovered, for 10 to 15 minutes or until fish flakes easily with a fork. Serve with lemon wedges. Serves 4.

Fried Grouper Sandwich

2 large eggs
½ tsp. salt
¼ tsp. cayenne pepper
1 cup flour, seasoned with salt and pepper to taste
1 cup cornmeal
4 6-oz. grouper fillets
Vegetable oil
Leaf lettuce
2 tomatoes, thinly sliced
8 soft sandwich rolls

Beat together eggs, salt, and cayenne pepper in a shallow dish. Place flour mixture and cornmeal in separate shallow dishes. Dredge each grouper fillet in flour mixture and dip in egg wash. Dredge fillets in cornmeal last. In a deep frying pan, heat 1 inch of oil to 375 degrees. Fry the fillets in batches for 2 to 4 minutes on each side or until browned and cooked through. Transfer fillets to paper towels to drain any excess oil. To serve, layer the lettuce, tomatoes, and fish on the sandwich rolls. Serves 4.

Fried Grouper Sandwich

Grouper Encrusted with Caramelized Onions

1 tsp. salt
1 tsp. black pepper
1 cup flour
3 tbsp. vegetable oil
1 cup diced onion
3 cloves garlic, minced
2 6-oz. skinless grouper fillets
½ cup dry vermouth
1 lemon
1 tbsp. butter

In a shallow dish, combine salt, black pepper, and flour. Heat vegetable oil in a sauté pan over high heat. Add onion and garlic to pan, and sauté until onions are translucent. Dredge the fish fillets in the seasoned flour. Lay the fillets on the sautéed onions and cook over high heat for 2 minutes. Using a spatula, turn the fillets, being careful to keep the caramelized onions attached to the fillets. Cook for 1 minute. Deglaze the pan with the vermouth. Squeeze the lemon over the fillets, then add the butter and let cook on high heat for 1 minute before serving. Serves 2.

Grouper Kiev

2 tbsp. chopped parsley
1 tbsp. lemon juice
¾ tsp. Worcestershire sauce
¼ tsp. hot sauce
1 clove garlic, minced
½ tsp. salt
Pepper to taste
½ cup butter, softened
2 lbs. grouper fillets
2 tbsp. water
2 eggs, beaten
½ cup flour
3 cups bread crumbs
Oil for frying

Work the parsley, lemon juice, Worcestershire sauce, hot sauce, garlic, salt, and pepper into the softened butter, and form into a roll using either plastic wrap or waxed paper. Chill until firm. Cut grouper fillets into serving-size portions. With a sharp knife, slice a pocket horizontally into each fillet. Cut the butter roll into the same number of portions as you have fillets. Place a portion in each grouper fillet pocket and secure with a toothpick. In a shallow dish, combine water and eggs. Roll fillets in flour, dip into eggs, and roll in bread crumbs, being sure to coat each fillet thoroughly. Chill for 1 hour. Fry in oil heated to 375 degrees for 2 to 3 minutes or until fillet turns golden brown. Drain on paper towels and serve immediately. Serves 6.

Grouper Creole

2 lbs. grouper fillets, thawed if frozen
1 tsp. Creole seasoning
½ cup butter

Cut fish fillets into 1-inch squares and coat with Creole seasoning. Melt butter in a frying pan. Add fish and cook until lightly brown. Turn and cook until other side is brown. Serves 8 (or 6 hungry fishermen).

Note: Tony Chachere's Creole Seasoning is my favorite, but others will work just as well.

Grouper Mediterranean

1 tbsp. olive oil
4 6-oz. grouper fillets
1 onion, chopped
2 cloves garlic, minced
¼ cup toasted almonds, chopped
½ cup dry white wine
⅓ cup clam juice or chicken stock
2 tbsp. lemon juice
1 tsp. thyme
1 tsp. marjoram
Black pepper to taste
3 tbsp. cilantro, chopped

In a nonstick sauté pan, heat oil over high heat. Sauté grouper fillets for 3 to 5 minutes until browned. Transfer fillets to a plate; set aside. Reduce heat to medium. Sauté onion and garlic for 4 to 5 minutes or until onion is tender. Add almonds, wine, clam juice or chicken stock, lemon juice, thyme, marjoram, and pepper to taste; bring to a boil, stirring frequently. Reduce heat to low. Cover pan and simmer for 10 minutes, stirring occasionally. Return fillets to pan and simmer until heated through. Serve fillets with additional sauce and topped with cilantro. Serves 4.

Grouper Parmesan

2 lbs. skinless grouper fillets, thawed if frozen
1 cup sour cream
¼ cup grated Parmesan cheese
1 tbsp. lemon juice
1 tbsp. grated onion
½ tsp. salt
⅛ tsp. hot sauce
Paprika to taste
Chopped parsley, for garnish

Preheat oven to 350 degrees. Cut grouper fillets into serving-size portions. Place in a well-greased 12 x 8-inch baking dish. In a small bowl, combine sour cream, Parmesan cheese, lemon juice, onion, salt, and hot sauce. Spread sour cream mixture over the fish. Sprinkle with paprika. Bake for 25 to 30 minutes or until fish flakes easily with a fork. Garnish with parsley. Serves 6.

Mackerel, King and Spanish

The beloved mackerels—Spanish and king—are welcomed in the northern gulf as harbingers of warmer weather and milder seas. They are pelagic fishes, long and slender with mouths full of sharp teeth and appetites that give even the most novice of fishermen a chance to bring home some dinner. The Spanish mackerel range from less than one pound to slightly more than ten pounds, while the king can grow to more than one hundred pounds.

The Spanish, with its gold spots, shows up first, surging along the outer sandbar and into cuts and bays all along the northern gulf coast. They follow the temperature line and the baitfish that comes with it. These mackerels are caught from jetties, piers, and on occasion from the shore. When the spring run is in full swing, fishermen often use multiple-hook rigs and catch two, three, or four at a time.

A few weeks later, the larger king mackerel put in their first appearance. They are a silvery-gray fish and tend not to have the gold spots, except for the very young ones. While these are almost never caught by shore or jetty fishermen, boat and pier fishermen catch them much the same way as they do the Spanish mackerel, but with somewhat larger bait.

Both are fatty fish, with a stronger flavor than lean fish. The Spanish is considered the better food fish, but because of the king's abundance and the bigger steaks and fillets, it too is popular table fare.

Captain's Choice

2 lbs. skin-on Spanish mackerel fillets, thawed
    if frozen
1 tsp. salt
¼ tsp. pepper
1 tbsp. butter, melted
½ cup mayonnaise or salad dressing
2 tbsp. ketchup
2 tbsp. prepared mustard

Sprinkle fish with salt and pepper. Place fish, skin-side down, on a well-greased broiler pan. Baste with butter. Broil approximately 4 inches from heat for 8 to 10 minutes. In a small bowl, combine mayonnaise, ketchup, and mustard. Spread mixture evenly over fish. Broil 4 to 5 additional minutes or until sauce bubbles and is lightly browned. Serves 6.

Grilled Spanish Mackerel

2 lbs. Spanish mackerel fillets, thawed if
    frozen
½ cup lemon juice
¼ cup olive oil
1 tsp. salt
1 tsp. oregano
¾ tsp. garlic salt
½ tsp. pepper

Make 4 or 5 shallow slits on skin side of each fish fillet. Place fish in shallow dish. In a small bowl, combine lemon juice, olive oil, salt, oregano, garlic salt, and pepper. Pour over fish and let marinate in the refrigerator for 30 minutes, turning once. Remove fish from marinade, reserving marinade for basting, and place in a well-greased, hinged wire grill. Cook approximately 4 inches from moderately hot coals for 4 to 5 minutes. Turn fish and baste with marinade. Cook for 4 to 5 additional minutes or until fish flakes easily with a fork. Serves 6.

Herb-Broiled Mackerel Steaks

4 small mackerel steaks
¼ cup butter, softened
1 tbsp. chopped fresh parsley
1 tbsp. thinly sliced green onion, including the
    tops
½ tsp. fresh tarragon, or ¼ tsp. dried tarragon
½ tsp. fresh thyme, or ¼ tsp. dried thyme
1 tsp. salt
⅛ tsp. freshly ground black pepper
⅛ tsp. paprika

Place fillets, skin-side down, in a well-greased broiler-safe pan without the rack. In small bowl, blend together butter, parsley, green onion, tarragon, thyme, salt, pepper, and paprika. Spread mixture over fillets. Broil about 4 inches from heat until fish flakes with a fork, about 8 to 10 minutes. Baste once or twice during cooking with pan juices. Serves 4.

Baked King Mackerel Steaks

2 lbs. 1-1¼-inch thick king mackerel steaks, thawed if frozen
1 tsp. salt
¼ tsp. pepper
¼ cup flour
Oil, for frying
1½ cups diced, seeded, and peeled tomatoes
1 cup fresh mushrooms, sliced
¼ cup dry vermouth
¼ tsp. crushed garlic
½ cup soft bread crumbs
2 tbsp. butter, melted

Preheat oven to 350 degrees. Sprinkle steaks with salt and pepper and roll in flour. Place steaks in a single layer in a 12-inch frying pan containing ⅛ inch of oil, hot but not smoking. Fry quickly over high heat for 3 to 4 minutes per side to brown steaks, turning carefully. Place steaks in a single layer in a well-greased 12 x 8-inch baking dish. In a 1-quart saucepan, combine tomatoes, mushrooms, vermouth, and garlic. Bring to a boil, stirring constantly. Pour hot sauce over fish. Combine bread crumbs and butter. Sprinkle bread crumb mixture over top of fish. Bake for 15 to 20 minutes or until fish flakes easily with a fork and crumbs are golden brown. Serves 6.

Tangy King Mackerel Steaks

2 lbs. king mackerel steaks, thawed if frozen
½ cup ketchup
¼ cup butter, melted
3 tbsp. lemon juice
2 tbsp. liquid smoke
2 tbsp. vinegar
1 tsp. salt
1 tsp. Worcestershire sauce
½ tsp. dry mustard
½ tsp. grated onion
¼ tsp. paprika
1 clove garlic, minced
3 drops hot sauce

Place fish in a shallow dish. In a separate bowl, combine remaining ingredients. Pour sauce over fish and let marinate in the refrigerator for 30 minutes, turning once. Remove fish, reserving sauce for basting. Place fish in a well-greased, hinged wire grill. Cook approximately 4 inches from moderately hot coals on an outdoor grill for 5 to 6 minutes. Turn fish and baste with sauce. Cook 7 to 10 minutes more or until fish flakes easily with a fork. Serves 6.

Baked King Mackerel Steaks

Marler Fish Cakes

1 lb. boneless king mackerel fillets, red streak
  removed
1 lb. baking potatoes
½ large green bell pepper, finely chopped
½ large onion, finely chopped
1 egg, beaten
Cajun seasoning to taste
Oil for frying

Boil fillets until they flake easily with a fork; remove from pot, reserving the water. Boil potato in reserved fish water until tender. In a large bowl, flake fish and combine with baking potato; mix with bell pepper and onion. Add egg to hold the mixture together. Shape the fish mixture into patties. Add Cajun seasoning to taste. Fry patties in oil in a hot skillet until browned on each side. Serves 4, but if you were a working fisherman, you would need a lot more.

Note: Scott Robinson, a Destin, Florida, charter captain, persuaded, after much time and effort, fellow fisherman Glen Marler to give him this recipe. Robinson said that Marler would bring the cakes for lunch, and, after sharing them with fellow fishermen, the recipe was soon in great demand. Marler has since passed away, but the recipe continues to be a prized one. This recipe has been handed down orally from Marler to Robinson to me. Because of its verbal history, the quantity of each ingredient has been estimated. The original recipe had no specific quantities. "It doesn't really matter much if you have more or less [of an ingredient]," explained Robinson. "It is a recipe that's hard to mess up."

Scott reported that every edible fish that swims in northern gulf waters can be substituted for king mackerel and that almost any seasoning that goes well with fish can be substituted for Cajun seasoning. "Mr. Marler," said Robinson, "was just a fan of Cajun seasoning."

Mullet

These are the white fish that you see leaping high out of the water as if jumping for pure joy. They are long, usually between one and two feet but occasionally growing to more than two feet in length. They swim in schools through bays and along the shore, where fishermen catch them in large cast nets. If a rod-and-reel fisherman catches a mullet, it is only because the fish had its mouth open in the wrong place at the wrong time. These fish don't normally take a baited hook.

Mullet are among the least expensive fish found in the fresh markets and are usually only available fresh, not frozen. Their flesh is quite oily, which gives mullet a strong flavor if it is kept around for a long time. Some shops offer smoked mullet, which is quite good if you like smoked fish.

Mullet also is a favorite baitfish, but it should be given consideration as a worthy panfish as well.

Onion-Baked Mullet

Mullet Shoestring Casserole

1 4-oz. can shoestring potatoes, divided
1 cup cooked, flaked mullet
1 10½-oz. can condensed cream of mushroom
   soup
1 5⅓-oz. can evaporated milk
1 3-oz. can sliced mushrooms, drained
¼ cup pimiento peppers
Parsley, for garnish

Preheat oven to 375 degrees. Set aside half of the shoestring potatoes. In a large bowl, combine mullet, remaining shoestring potatoes, cream of mushroom soup, evaporated milk, sliced mushrooms, and pimientos. Pour mixture into a well-greased 1½-quart baking dish. Arrange reserved potatoes on top. Bake, uncovered, for 20 to 25 minutes or until thoroughly heated. Garnish with parsley. Serves 4.

Onion-Baked Mullet

2 lbs. skinless mullet fillets, thawed if frozen
1 tsp. salt
1 cup sour cream
1 cup mayonnaise or salad dressing
1 ⁴⁄₁₀-oz. package Ranch salad dressing mix
2 3-oz. cans French-fried onions, crushed

Preheat oven to 350 degrees. Cut fish into serving-size portions. Sprinkle with salt. In a small bowl, combine sour cream, mayonnaise, and Ranch salad dressing mix. Dip fish in sour cream mixture followed by crushed French-fried onions. Place fish on a well-greased 15 x 9-inch baking pan. Bake for 20 to 25 minutes or until fish flakes easily with a fork. Serves 6.

Mullet Casserole Panacea

½ cup chopped green pepper
2 tbsp. butter
2 tbsp. flour
¼ tsp. oregano
½ tsp. salt
⅛ tsp. pepper
1 cup half-and-half
⅔ cup cheddar cheese, divided
2 cups cooked, flaked mullet
½ cup bread crumbs

Preheat oven to 450 degrees. Cook green pepper in butter in a large saucepan until tender. Reduce heat; stir in flour, oregano, salt, and pepper. Gradually add half-and-half and cook until thickened. Add ⅓ cup cheese, stirring constantly until cheese melts. Fold in fish, mixing well. Spoon into 4 ramekins. Combine remaining ⅓ cup cheese and bread crumbs; sprinkle over top of casseroles. Bake for 5 minutes or until bubbly. Serves 4.

Mullet in Coral Sauce

2 lbs. skin-on mullet fillets, thawed if frozen
½ cup butter, melted
2 tbsp. lemon juice
1 tsp. grated onion
1 tsp. paprika
1 tsp. salt
⅛ tsp. pepper

Preheat oven to 350 degrees. Place fish in a single layer, skin-side down, in a well-greased 12 x 8-inch baking dish. In a separate bowl, combine remaining ingredients. Pour sauce over fish. Bake for 20 to 25 minutes or until fish flakes easily with a fork. Serves 6.

Smoked Mullet

2 lbs. skinless mullet fillets
⅓ cup soy sauce
3 tbsp. cooking oil
1 tbsp. liquid smoke
1 clove garlic, minced
½ tsp. ginger
½ tsp. salt
Lemon wedges, for garnish

Cut mullet into serving-size portions. Combine soy sauce, cooking oil, liquid smoke, garlic, ginger, and salt; mix thoroughly. Place fish on a well-greased broiler pan; brush with sauce. Broil about 3 inches from source of heat for 4 to 6 minutes. Turn carefully and brush other side with sauce. Broil for about 4 to 6 more minutes, basting occasionally, until fish flakes easily with a fork. Serve with lemon wedges. Serves 6.

Note: Long-time coastal fishermen who have made an art form out of smoked mullet might be a little skeptical of a "quick version." However, this is an excellent recipe that can be made in much less time than the traditional smoking method.

Any fish with a high oil content is suitable for smoking. Just be sure to baste it often with cooking oil to keep it moist.

Smoky Mullet Salad

1½ lbs. skinless and boneless smoked mullet
6 cups salad greens, broken into pieces
1½ cups green peas, cooked and drained
1 cup julienned Swiss cheese
1 cup thinly sliced red onion
⅓ cup mayonnaise
1 tbsp. sugar
¾ tsp. salt
¼ tsp. pepper
3 slices cooked bacon, crumbled
6 cherry tomatoes

Flake the fish. In a large bowl, combine fish, salad greens, peas, cheese, and onion. Chill. In a separate bowl, combine mayonnaise, sugar, salt, and pepper. Pour dressing over salad; toss lightly. Sprinkle with bacon and top with cherry tomatoes. Serve immediately. Serves 6.

Pompano

Pompano tend to be found in northern gulf waters for most of the year. They attract the most attention from fishermen when they gather into schools and roam the shoreline for sand fleas and other small-shelled animals in spring, fall, and early winter. They are a frustration to the casual fisherman because they are so good at spotting hooked bait. The seasoned pompano angler is rewarded more frequently in landing one of the gulf's tastiest fish.

There are several pompano species in the northern gulf, but the most common is the Florida pompano, which reaches about seven or eight pounds. This fish is silvery with a slight yellow cast and forked tail. It can be purchased in fresh markets, where it frequently will be one of the highest-priced fish in the case.

Pompano in Foil

6 pan-dressed pompano, thawed if frozen
1 tsp. salt
⅛ tsp. pepper
3 oz. mushrooms, chopped, drained if canned
½ cup dry white wine
¼ cup butter, melted
3 tbsp. finely chopped green onion
3 tbsp. lime juice
1 tbsp. chopped parsley
2½ oz. whole button mushrooms, drained if
   canned

Preheat oven to 350 degrees. Pat pompano dry with a paper towel. Sprinkle the inside flesh with salt and pepper. Cut 6 pieces of heavy-duty aluminum foil into 18-inch squares; grease lightly. Place each fish on a separate piece of foil. In a small bowl, combine chopped mushrooms, white wine, butter, green onion, lime juice, and parsley. Pour sauce over the fish. Place 2 button mushrooms on each fish. Wrap foil up over the fish and close all edges with tight double folds. Bake for 50 minutes or until fish flakes easily with a fork. Serves 6.

Kiev-Style Pompano

4-6 ½-lb. pan-dressed pompano
2 tsp. salt, divided
⅛ tsp. pepper
7 tbsp. butter, divided
1 cup chopped parsley
1 egg, beaten
¼ cup milk
¾ cup dry bread crumbs
¾ cup grated Swiss cheese

Preheat oven to 500 degrees. Sprinkle fish inside and out with 1 tsp. salt and pepper. Soften 4 tbsp. butter and add parsley; mix thoroughly. Spread inside of each fish with parsley butter. In a shallow dish, combine egg, milk, and remaining 1 tsp. salt. In a separate dish, combine bread crumbs and cheese. Dip fish in egg mixture and immediately roll in breadcrumb mixture. Place on a well-greased 15 x 12-inch baking sheet. Sprinkle remaining bread crumb mixture over fish. Melt remaining 3 tbsp. butter and drizzle over the fish. Bake for 15 to 20 minutes or until fish flakes easily with a fork. Serves 4 to 6.

Baked Pompano Fillets

2 lbs. pompano fillets, thawed if frozen
1 tsp. salt
⅛ tsp. pepper
¼ cup butter, melted
2 tbsp. lemon juice
1 tsp. grated onion
⅛ tsp. paprika

Preheat oven to 350 degrees. Sprinkle fillets with salt and pepper. Place in a single layer in a well-greased 18 x 14-inch baking pan. In a small dish, combine butter, lemon juice, onion, and paprika. Cover fillets with the sauce. Bake for 20 to 25 minutes or until fish flakes easily with a fork. Serves 6.

Florida Pompano Amandine

½ cup sliced almonds
¾ cup butter, melted, divided
4 6-oz. Florida pompano fillets
2 tsp. cayenne pepper
Sea salt to taste
Ground black pepper to taste
1 cup rice flour
¼ cup lemon juice
¼ cup chopped flat leaf parsley

Heat oven to 375 degrees. Place sliced almonds and ¼ cup butter in an ovenproof dish; toast for 7 minutes or until golden. Remove from oven and set aside. Sprinkle pompano fillets with cayenne, sea salt, and pepper, then dredge in rice flour. In a shallow skillet over medium-high heat, add remaining ½ cup butter and fish fillets. Cook for 3 to 5 minutes per side until cooked through. Remove fillets from pan and keep warm. Add toasted almonds, lemon juice, and parsley to the butter in the skillet, mix well, and spoon over cooked fillets. Serves 4.

Pompano with Tomatoes

2 lbs. skinless pompano fillets
2 tbsp. grated onion
1 tsp. salt
⅛ tsp. pepper
2 tomatoes, cut into small pieces
¼ cup butter
1 cup shredded Swiss cheese

Place fillets in a single layer in a microwave-safe dish, with thicker fillets to the outside of dish. Sprinkle fillets with onion, salt, and pepper. Top fillets with tomatoes, dot with butter, and sprinkle with cheese. Cook, uncovered, in the microwave on high for 8 to 10 minutes or until fish flakes easily with a fork; rotate dish once during cooking. Serves 6.

Florida Pompano Amandine

Shark

The northern gulf is home to close to two dozen sharks. If you happen to see one while you are playing in the surf, it is almost certain that you won't know what kind it is— you probably won't wait around long enough to do that. The features that you most likely will remember are the triangular fin on the back, the forked tail, and—usually—a pointy nose.

Sharks eat almost anything, so fishermen catch them in a variety of ways and in a variety of locations: reefs, bays, inlets, jetties, piers, and in the surf. In fact, a common activity for visitors to the coast is to fish for sharks from the shore at night. A number of sharks are caught that way, including a good number of large ones, some exceeding one hundred pounds.

Sharks generally are considered of sufficient food quality that most fresh markets will carry shark steaks for at least part of the year. Fishermen need to be aware of two things: First, some sharks are protected by law because their populations are low, and so there could be a fine associated with keeping one in the cooler. You need to be sure which kinds you can and cannot keep. Second, the urea in shark flesh turns to ammonia fairly quickly after a shark dies. Bleed and dress the shark as soon as possible after catching it.

One nice thing about the shark is that except for the jaws, there are no bones, just cartilage. So, there is plenty of boneless flesh to enjoy.

Baked Shark with Mushrooms

1½ lbs. skinless shark fillets, thawed if frozen
½ tsp. salt
¼ tsp. pepper
½ cup condensed cream of celery soup
1 cup sliced fresh mushrooms
¼ cup dry white wine
1 cup grated sharp Cheddar cheese
Parsley, for garnish

Preheat oven to 350 degrees. Cut shark fillets into serving-size portions. Place fish in a single layer in a well-greased, 1½-quart shallow casserole dish. Sprinkle with salt and pepper. In a separate dish, combine cream of celery soup, mushrooms, and wine. Spread soup mixture over fish. Sprinkle with cheese. Cover and bake for 20 to 25 minutes or until fish flakes easily with a fork. Garnish with parsley. Serves 4.

Batter-Fried Shark

2 lbs. shark fillets
1 cup flour
1 tbsp. salt
1 tsp. baking powder
1 cup water
1 tbsp. vinegar
Vegetable oil, for frying

Cut shark into 1-inch cubes. In a bowl, combine flour, salt, and baking powder. Slowly add water and vinegar; mix well. Dip fish cubes into batter, being sure to coat thoroughly. Carefully drop into hot oil heated to approximately 425 degrees. Cook for 2 to 3 minutes or until golden brown. Serves 6.

Shark Italiano

1½ lbs. skinless shark fillets, thawed if frozen
½ tsp. salt
¼ tsp. pepper
1 16-oz. can stewed tomatoes
1 clove garlic, minced
1 cup grated mozzarella cheese
Parsley, for garnish

Preheat oven to 350 degrees. Cut shark fillets into serving-size portions. Place fish in a single layer in a well-greased 1½-quart shallow casserole dish. Sprinkle with salt and pepper. Combine tomatoes and garlic; spread over fish. Sprinkle with cheese. Bake for 20 to 25 minutes or until fish flakes easily with a fork. Garnish with parsley. Serves 4.

Shark in a Tomato and Citrus Sauce

1 lb. skinless shark fillets, cut into 6 pieces
1 tsp. salt
¼ cup olive oil, divided
3 cloves garlic, crushed
8 sprigs coriander
6 tbsp. puréed tomato
2 tbsp. fresh lemon or lime juice
1 tsp. dried red chili peppers
⅓ cup water

Preheat oven to 425 degrees. Rub salt well onto shark pieces. Use a small amount of oil to coat a shallow baking dish, and place shark in the baking dish. Heat the remaining oil in a skillet and gently fry the garlic. Add the coriander. Once the coriander is aromatic, add the puréed tomato and lemon or lime juice. Stir to combine. Pour tomato-citrus sauce over the shark. Sprinkle the chili peppers over the shark and add water to the baking dish. Bake for 20 to 25 minutes. Serves 2-3.

Shark Italiano

Broiled Shark with Orange Butter

1½ lbs. skinless shark fillets, thawed if frozen
¾ tsp. salt
¼ tsp. pepper
3 tbsp. orange juice concentrate
3 tbsp. butter, melted
Orange slices, for garnish
Parsley, for garnish

Cut shark fillets into serving-size portions. Place fish in a single layer in a well-greased 1½-quart shallow casserole dish. Sprinkle with salt and pepper. Combine orange juice concentrate and butter. Pour over fish. Broil approximately 4 inches from heat source for 4 to 6 minutes. Turn fish and baste with orange butter in the pan. Broil for 6 to 8 additional minutes or until fish flakes easily with a fork. Garnish with orange slices and parsley. Serves 4.

Shark en Papillote

2 lbs. shark fillets, thawed if frozen
1 tsp. salt
⅛ tsp. pepper
1 tbsp. flour
1 cup sliced onion
1 cup sliced green pepper
¼ cup butter, melted
2 tbsp. lemon juice
Paprika to taste
Lemon wedges, for garnish

Preheat oven to 350 degrees. Cut shark into serving-size portions. Sprinkle with salt and pepper. Place flour in a 16 x 10-inch brown paper oven bag and shake to coat the inside to protect the bag from bursting. Place bag in a 12 x 8-inch baking dish. Place fish in the bag. Arrange onion and green pepper on top of the fish. Combine butter and lemon juice; pour over fish. Close end of bag loosely with the tie that came with the bag. Puncture 6 ½-inch slits in the top of the bag. Bake for 20 to 25 minutes or until fish flakes easily with a fork. Allow bag to cool slightly removing fish and transferring to a warm serving platter. Sprinkle with paprika and serve with lemon wedges. Serves 6.

Note: This dish is quite popular with pompano as well. The pompano is more often in pan-dressed form rather than fillets.

Sheepshead

The black vertical bars against a white and gray background and the big front teeth make the sheepshead an easy fish to identify. It can be caught year-round but is particularly sought-after in colder months, when many of the pelagic species have departed for warmer climates. Sheepshead seem to particularly like hanging around bridge pilings, jetties, and sea walls, where they feast on barnacles, crunching the hard shells with those formidable teeth.

The sheepshead ranges from panfish-size to more than ten pounds. Fresh markets carry them from time to time, and skilled fishermen can fill a stringer if they know the trick of setting the hook on these notorious bait stealers. Some old hands joke that you have to know how to set the hook just before the sheepshead bites.

They are an excellent food fish, but scales and strong bones make cleaning them a daunting task.

Broiled Sheepshead

2 lbs. sheepshead fillets
¼ cup vegetable oil
1 tsp. salt
⅛ tsp. pepper
2 4-oz. cans chopped mushrooms, drained
1 cup grated cheddar cheese
2 tbsp. fresh parsley, chopped

Cut fish into serving-size pieces. Combine oil, salt, and pepper; mix thoroughly. In a separate bowl, combine mushrooms, cheese, and parsley. Place fish on lightly greased broiler pan and brush with seasoned oil. Broil about 3 inches from heat source for 3 to 4 minutes. Turn carefully and brush fish with remaining oil. Broil for 3 to 4 additional minutes or until fish flakes easily with a fork. Spread mushroom mixture on fish and broil for 2 to 3 minutes or until light brown. Serves 6.

Sheepshead Chowder

1 lb. skinless sheepshead fillets, thawed if
    frozen
½ cup chopped onion
2 tbsp. butter or oil
2 cups diced potatoes
1 cup boiling water
¾ tsp. salt
Pepper to taste
2 cups milk
1 8-oz. can cream-style yellow corn
Chopped parsley, for garnish

Cut fish fillets into 1-inch squares. In a 3-quart saucepan, cook onion in butter until tender but not brown. Add potatoes, water, salt, and pepper to saucepan. Cover and simmer for 10 minutes. Add fish and simmer for 5 to 10 minutes more or until fish flakes easily with a fork and potatoes are tender. Add the milk and corn. Heat thoroughly, but do not boil. Garnish with parsley. Serve hot. Serves 4.

2 lbs. sheepshead fillets, thawed if frozen
1½ tsp. salt, divided
¼ tsp. pepper
3 slices bacon, chopped
1 cup chopped fresh mushrooms
¼ cup minced onion
¼ cup minced celery
2 cups wild rice, cooked according to package
   directions
2 tbsp. butter, melted
Mushroom-Walnut Sauce

Mushroom-Walnut Sauce

1 cup sliced fresh mushrooms
1 tbsp. minced onion
3 tbsp. butter, melted
3 tbsp. flour
½ tsp. dry mustard
½ tsp. salt
¼ tsp. thyme
2 cups half-and-half
¼ cup walnuts, toasted

Preheat oven to 350 degrees. Cut fish into serving-sized portions and season with 1 tsp. salt and pepper. In a 10-inch frying pan, cook bacon until lightly browned. Add mushrooms, onion, and celery and cook until tender. Stir in cooked rice and remaining ½ tsp. salt. Place fish in a well-greased 12 x 8-inch baking pan. Spoon rice mixture over the top of the fish. Drizzle butter over the rice. Cover and bake for 20 minutes or until fish flakes easily with a fork. Serve with Mushroom-Walnut Sauce. Serves 6.

In a 1-quart saucepan, cook mushrooms and onion in butter until tender. Stir in flour, mustard, salt, and thyme. Add half-and-half gradually and cook until thick and smooth, stirring constantly. Add walnuts; cook until heated through. Makes approximately 2½ cups sauce.

Sheepshead Macadamia

½ cup flour
2 large eggs
2 cups macadamia nuts, finely chopped
6 6-oz. sheepshead fillets
Salt to taste
Ground black pepper to taste
4 tbsp. olive oil

Place flour in a shallow plate. Whisk eggs in a small bowl until blended. Place macadamia nuts on another shallow plate. Sprinkle fish with salt and pepper. Coat fillets with flour; dip into eggs, then coat fillets with macadamia nuts. Heat oil in a heavy, large skillet over medium heat. Place fillets in skillet; cook for 4 minutes per side until golden brown and opaque in the center. Serves 6.

Sheepshead Onion Bake

2 lbs. sheepshead fillets, thawed if frozen
3 cups sliced onion
2 tbsp. butter, melted
1 tsp. salt
½ cup mayonnaise
¼ cup grated Parmesan cheese
2 tbsp. lemon juice
1 tsp. Worcestershire sauce
½ tsp. paprika
Oregano to taste

Preheat oven to 350 degrees. Cut fish into serving-size portions. Cook onion in butter until tender. Spread onion over the bottom of a shallow 2-quart baking dish. Place fish on top of onion. Combine mayonnaise, cheese, lemon juice, Worcestershire sauce, and paprika; mix well. Spread mayonnaise mixture evenly over the fish. Bake for 20 minutes or until fish flakes easily with a fork. Sprinkle with oregano. Serves 6.

Snappers

These are the fish that every fisherman wants to catch and that no fresh market can do without. The signature snapper is the red snapper, but it is certainly not the only fine food fish labeled "snapper" in the northern gulf region. Of the true snappers, there are also the vermilion, lane, and gray (or black) snappers. Plus, there are several porgy species that northern gulf fishermen lump into a group that they call white snapper. All are reef fish typically caught with live or dead bait. Some, such as the red snapper, top out around forty pounds while the gray is lucky to reach fifteen pounds and the vermilion—commonly called a beeliner or mingo—might make ten pounds on a good day.

Snappers have length and creel limits because of the fishing pressure on this group of fish, and there are ongoing discussions between the regulatory groups and fishermen about whether those limits are too tight or too loose. In some parts of the northern gulf, the limits have allowed the snapper population to rebound so rapidly that, in the past few years, it has become the easiest and predominant catch of bottom fishermen, particularly in Alabama coastal waters. The arguments over these limits are certain to continue. Many fishermen expect both the length, creel and season limits to be eased, but it is difficult to estimate as to what degree.

All snappers are excellent food fish and can be found on most seafood restaurant menus throughout the northern gulf.

Baked Stuffed Snapper Fillets

2 lbs. snapper fillets, thawed if frozen
1 tsp. salt
¼ tsp. pepper
1 tsp. chicken stock base, dissolved in ⅓ cup
    boiling water
4 slices whole wheat bread, diced
2 tbsp. chopped parsley
2 tbsp. chopped onion
2 tsp. chives
¼ tsp. garlic powder
¼ tsp. poultry seasoning
2 tbsp. butter, melted
Paprika to taste

Preheat oven to 350 degrees. Sprinkle fish with salt and pepper. In a large bowl, combine chicken stock, bread, parsley, onion, chives, garlic powder, and poultry seasoning. Mix well. Place half of the fish, skin-side down, in a 12 x 8-inch well-greased baking dish. Place stuffing on top of fish and cover with remaining fish, skin-side up. Baste fish with butter and sprinkle with paprika. Bake for 25 to 30 minutes or until fish flakes easily with a fork. Serves 6.

Emerald Coast Snapper

1 lb. snapper fillets, thawed if frozen
3 tsp. Dijon mustard, divided
4 dried apricots, finely chopped
3 tbsp. minced celery
2 tbsp. toasted, slivered almonds
¾ tsp. white pepper
¾ cup unsweetened orange juice
¾ cup chicken broth
½ tsp. curry powder
2 tsp. cornstarch
1 tbsp. dry sherry

Spread the inside of the fish fillets with 2 tsp. Dijon mustard. Combine apricots, celery, almonds, and ¼ tsp. white pepper; mix well. Divide mixture on top of fillets. Roll up fillets, secure with a toothpick, and stand on its end. Combine orange juice, chicken broth, remaining 1 tsp. Dijon mustard, remaining ½ tsp. white pepper, and curry powder in a 10-inch frying pan; bring to a simmer. Lower fillets, seam side down, in simmering liquid; cover and simmer for 5 to 6 minutes; turn fillets. Simmer for 3 to 5 more minutes. With a slotted spatula, transfer fillets to a warm platter. Boil remaining liquid until mixture reduces to 1 cup. Combine cornstarch and sherry; mix well and stir into poaching liquid. Boil, stirring constantly, for 1 minute. Remove toothpicks and discard; spoon sauce over fillets. Serves 4.

Pan-Fried White Snapper

3 lbs. whole, dressed white snapper
Cooking oil
½ cup cornmeal, white stone-ground if
   available, plus additional if needed
Butter
Salt, pepper, and lemon juice to taste

Wash snapper and remove excess moisture by patting dry with a paper towel. Place a handful of cornmeal in a strong paper or plastic sack, followed by the fish, one or two at a time. Shake to coat the fish. Heat oil in a skillet until hot. Shake excess cornmeal off of fish and place in skillet. Adjust heat so that fish fry quickly but do not burn. Cook until the edges of the fish are crisp and brown; turn over. Cook for 2 to 3 minutes more to brown the second side. Remove cooked fish and place on a paper towel to drain excess oil. Immediately run a pat of butter over each fish and sprinkle with salt, pepper, and lemon juice to taste. Serve immediately. Serves 8.

Pan-Grilled Snapper with Avocado-Strawberry Salsa

1 jalapeño pepper, finely chopped
1 ripe avocado, diced
2 cups chopped strawberries
¼ cup chopped red onion
2 tbsp. chopped cilantro
1 tsp. fresh lime juice
¼ tsp. sugar
Sea salt to taste
4 6-oz. snapper fillets
1 tbsp. olive oil
1½ tbsp. lime zest

Stir jalapeño, avocado, strawberries, red onion, cilantro, lime juice, sugar, and sea salt together in a bowl. Cover and set aside. Preheat a stovetop grill pan over high heat. Pat snapper fillets dry, then brush both sides with the oil. Sprinkle with lime zest. Lay fillets on grill pan, skin-side down, and cook for 4 to 5 minutes on each side until cooked through. Transfer fillets to plates and top with avocado-strawberry salsa. Serves 4.

Note: The salsa may be made several hours ahead and chilled. If preparing in advance, omit the avocado, sugar, and salt until just before serving.

Pan-Grilled Snapper with Avocado-Strawberry Salsa

Florida Red Snapper

2 lbs. red snapper fillets, thawed if frozen
¼ cup grated onion
2 tbsp. lemon juice
2 tbsp. orange juice
2 tsp. grated orange peel
½ tsp. salt
⅛ tsp. nutmeg
⅛ tsp. pepper

Cut snapper fillets into 6 portions. Place in a single layer, skin-side down, in a well-greased 12 x 8-inch baking dish. Combine onion, lemon juice, orange juice, orange peel, and salt. Pour over fish, cover, and marinate in the refrigerator for 30 minutes. Preheat oven to 350 degrees. Sprinkle fish with nutmeg and pepper. Bake for 25 to 30 minutes or until fish flakes easily with a fork. Serves 6.

Horseradish-Crusted Snapper

⅓ cup mayonnaise
2 tbsp. horseradish
1 tbsp. bread crumbs
½ tsp. minced garlic
1 anchovy fillet, optional
1 pinch white pepper
4 6-oz. snapper fillets
Flour to coat

Preheat oven to 350 degrees. Blend mayonnaise, horseradish, bread crumbs, garlic, anchovy, and pepper in a food processor. Dredge snapper in flour, then coat with horseradish mixture. Bake for 9 to 12 minutes or until fish flakes easily with a fork. Serves 4.

Scrumptious Broiled Snapper

2 lbs. snapper fillets
¼ cup vegetable oil
1 tsp. salt
⅛ tsp. pepper
2 4-oz. cans mushroom stems and pieces,
    drained and chopped
1 cup grated Cheddar cheese
2 tbsp. chopped parsley

Cut fish into serving-size pieces. In a small bowl, combine oil, salt, and pepper; mix thoroughly. In a separate dish, combine mushrooms, cheese, and parsley. Place fish on a lightly oiled broiler pan and brush with seasoned oil. Broil for about 3 inches from heat source for 3 to 4 minutes. Turn carefully and brush fish with remaining oil. Broil for an additional 3 to 4 minutes or until fish flakes easily when tested with a fork. Spread mushroom mixture on fish and broil for 2 to 3 minutes or until light brown. Serves 6.

Snapper Boca Chica

1½ lbs. snapper fillets
1½ cups orange juice
½ cup lime juice
½ cup honey
2 tsp. paprika
1 tsp. salt

Score the top of the snapper fillets with 6 shallow cuts in a large checkerboard pattern. Combine orange juice, lime juice, and honey in a flat-bottomed container and mix well. Place fish in container with juice mixture and marinate for 1 hour in the refrigerator. Combine paprika and salt. Place fish on a broiler pan and apply paprika mixture to the top of fillets. Broil 10 minutes for each inch of thickness or until fish flakes easily with a fork. While fish is cooking, boil marinade for 5 minutes and use to baste fish just before removing from the oven. Serves 4.

Note: This dish works best with red snapper, vermilion snapper, or lane snapper.

Snapper Scampi

2 tbsp. olive oil
2 tbsp. butter
2 garlic cloves, minced
1 medium tomato, finely chopped
2 tbsp. chopped parsley
2 tbsp. lemon juice
½ tsp. oregano
Salt and pepper to taste
1 lb. snapper fillets, cut into serving-size
    portions

Preheat oven to 400 degrees. Combine oil, butter, and garlic in a saucepan; stir until butter is melted. When the ingredients are well blended, pour the mixture into a bowl and add the tomato, parsley, lemon juice, oregano, salt, and pepper. Place the snapper fillets in a single layer on a lightly greased baking dish. Pour the butter mixture evenly over the fillets. Place the baking dish in the oven. Bake for 5 to 8 minutes, or until fish flakes easily with a fork. Serves 4.

Sunshine Snapper

2 lbs. snapper fillets
3 tbsp. butter, melted
2 tbsp. orange juice
2 tsp. grated orange peel
1 tsp. salt
⅛ tsp. nutmeg
⅛ tsp. pepper

Preheat oven to 350 degrees. Cut fish into 6 pieces. Place in a single layer in a lightly oiled baking dish. Combine remaining ingredients; pour over fish. Bake for 20 to 25 minutes or until fish flakes easily with a fork. Serves 6.

Swordfish

Fresh swordfish is more likely to be found at a market than on a fisherman's hook in the northern gulf. They are a deep-water fish and roam far offshore, where only the fisherman with plenty of time and money will have a chance to catch his own.

Easily identified by the sword-like snout, the swordfish is large—sometimes nearing fifteen feet—and considered a prime food fish. Grilled swordfish steaks are a prized meal.

Apricot-Glazed Swordfish

4 cups orange juice
2 tsp. minced fresh ginger
1 cinnamon stick
1 cup apricot preserves
4 5-oz. portions swordfish
Kosher salt to taste
White pepper to taste
Olive oil, as needed

In a small saucepan over medium-high heat, add orange juice, ginger, and cinnamon stick. Reduce mixture by 70 percent. Whisk in apricot preserves, making sure to melt out any lumps. Strain mixture through a fine mesh sieve into a bowl and reserve for future use. Preheat oven to 375 degrees. Heat a large skillet over medium-high heat. Season swordfish on both sides with salt and pepper. Add oil to pan. When pan generates a small amount of smoke, place fillets into the pan. When fish is golden brown, flip over and cook for 20 seconds. Place swordfish on a greased sheet pan, browned-side up, and liberally coat with the apricot glaze. Place in the oven. About 1 minute before the swordfish is completely opaque in the center, apply another coat of the apricot glaze and return to oven until opaque. Serves 4.

Teriyaki Swordfish

2 lbs. swordfish steaks
½ cup teriyaki sauce
2 tbsp. butter, melted

Marinate swordfish in teriyaki sauce for 5 to 7 minutes on each side. Place steaks on a lightly oiled grill over medium heat. Grill steaks for approximately 5 minutes per side or until the fish flakes easily with a fork, basting regularly with melted butter. Serves 6 to 8.

Note: Some cooks like to sprinkle the steaks with garlic powder while grilling. Others enjoy serving the steaks with slices of pineapple that are briefly placed on the grill before serving. Both are delicious variations!

Teriyaki Swordfish

Grilled Swordfish

2 lbs. swordfish steaks
¼ cup orange juice
¼ cup soy sauce
2 tbsp. ketchup
2 tbsp. vegetable oil
2 tbsp. chopped parsley
1 tbsp. lemon juice
1 clove garlic, minced
½ tsp. pepper

Cut swordfish into serving-size portions and place in shallow baking dish in a single layer. Combine remaining ingredients and pour over steaks. Refrigerate for 30 minutes, turning fish once. Remove fish from marinade. Heat marinade to a boil, then remove from heat. Place fish on lightly oiled, hinged wire grill. Cook 4 inches from moderately hot coals for 5 to 6 minutes. Turn fish, baste with marinade, and cook 4 to 5 minutes longer or until internal steak temperature reaches 140 degrees. Serves 6.

Tilefish

The several species of this deep-water fish are all excellent food fare—so good, in fact, that one Panama City Beach, Florida, restaurant consistently listed tilefish as its catch of the day for a number of years.

Fresh markets carry tilefish when they can get them. Some of the two-day charter boat trips to very deep water reward their fishermen with a catch of tilefish.

These long fish are usually gold in color with patterned sides fading to white on the belly. They can reach more than three feet in length and weigh more than fifty pounds.

Ybor City Fillet

1½ lbs. tilefish fillets
½ cup diced yellow bell pepper
½ cup diced green bell pepper
2 cups cooked yellow rice
1 tbsp. paprika
2 tsp. minced garlic
1 tsp. black pepper
1 tsp. salt
1 tsp. ground cumin

Cut fish into 2-inch cubes. Mix bell peppers with cooked rice; set aside and keep warm. In a mixing bowl, combine paprika, garlic, pepper, salt, cumin, and fish. Spread over fish until coated well. Place fish on a lightly oiled broiler pan and broil 4 to 6 inches from heat 5 for to 6 minutes on each side, or until fish flakes easily with a fork. Serve with the rice. Serves 4.

Herb-Roasted Tilefish

4 tilefish fillets
1 oz. lemon oil
1 tsp. minced fresh chives
1 tsp. minced fresh rosemary
Sea salt to taste
Freshly ground black pepper to taste

Preheat oven to 400 degrees. Season the fish by rubbing lemon oil over the flesh and skin. Season with chives, rosemary sea salt, and black pepper. Place on a sheet pan, skin-side down, and roast for 12 to 15 minutes or until fish flakes easily with a fork. Serves 4.

Ybor City Fillet

Tilefish Excelsior

1 stick butter
1½ cups mushrooms, sliced
3 canned artichoke bottoms, sliced
¼ cup chopped parsley
¼ cup red wine
4 tilefish fillets
Salt and pepper to taste
¼ cup flour
1 tbsp. lemon juice

Brown the butter. Add mushrooms and artichoke bottoms and sauté until tender. Add parsley and wine; toss lightly. Season tilefish with salt and pepper and coat in flour. Pan-fry until fish is brown and flakes easily with a fork. Top fish with lemon juice and mushroom mixture. Serves 4.

Tilefish Torney

1½ lbs. tilefish fillets
3 tbsp. butter
3 tbsp. flour
1 tsp. thyme
½ tsp. summer savory
½ tsp. marjoram
2 cups milk
⅓ cup grated cheddar cheese
¼ tsp. hot sauce

Preheat oven to 350 degrees. Cut fish into serving-size portions. Melt butter in a saucepan; blend in flour, thyme, savory, and marjoram. Gradually add milk and cook until mixture thickens, stirring constantly. Remove from heat; stir in cheese and hot sauce. Place fish in baking dish and cover with sauce. Bake for 15 to 20 minutes or until fish flakes easily with a fork. Serves 6.

Triggerfish

There was a time not long ago that fishermen and charter boat captains cursed the triggerfish. It was a bait stealer and raced to hooks baited for red snapper. Its hide is like leather, and its sharp teeth and nasty disposition left many a fisherman with scars and stories to tell. The common practice once was to kill the triggerfish and throw it back. Somewhere along the line, someone decided to see what was underneath that tough gray hide. What they discovered was delectable white meat. Today, it commands a high price in the fresh markets, and fishermen in recent years have targeted it so much that the government has established season, creel, and length limits for triggerfish.

These reef fish are usually found in the same places as snapper and can be easily caught with almost any kind of dead bait, but they occasionally are caught around jetties and structure in bays.

With a sharp knife, they are not nearly so hard to clean as once was thought—and the reward is worth it. This extremely lean fish can be kept for months in the freezer without any loss of quality.

Baked Triggerfish with Vegetables

1½ lbs. triggerfish fillets, thawed if frozen
½ tsp. salt
¼ tsp. pepper
2 cups mixed vegetables, precooked
1 12-oz. jar home-style gravy with onion
Parsley, for garnish

Preheat oven to 350 degrees. Cut fillets into serving-size portions. Place fish in a single layer in a well-greased 1½-quart shallow casserole dish. Sprinkle with salt and pepper. In a 1-quart bowl, combine vegetables with gravy; spread over fish. Cover and bake for 20 to 25 minutes or until fish flakes easily with a fork. Garnish with parsley. Serves 4.

Note: No matter how the precooked vegetables are prepared, they simply shouldn't be raw when used in this recipe.

Batter-Fried Triggerfish

2 lbs. triggerfish fillets, thawed if frozen
1 cup flour
1 tbsp. salt
1 tsp. baking powder
1 cup water
1 tbsp. vinegar
Oil for frying

Cut fillets into 1-inch cubes. Combine flour, salt, and baking powder. Slowly add water and vinegar; mix well. Dip fish cubes into batter and drop into oil heated to approximately 425 degrees. Cook for 2 to 3 minutes or until golden brown. Drain on paper towels. Serves 6.

Easy Triggerfish and Broccoli Casserole

1¼ cups broccoli spears, steamed
1 cup cooked, flaked triggerfish
½ cup milk
1 10¾-oz. can condensed cream of
   mushroom soup
¼ tsp. salt
⅛ tsp. pepper
½ cup crushed potato chips
Parsley, for garnish

Preheat oven to 425 degrees. Place broccoli in a single layer in a well-greased, 1½-quart shallow casserole dish. In a separate dish, combine fish, milk, soup, salt, and pepper. Spread fish mixture over broccoli. Sprinkle potato chips over the top of the fish mixture. Bake for 10 to 12 minutes or until heated through Garnish with parsley. Serves 4.

Grilled Triggerfish Tangerine

4 6-oz. triggerfish fillets
2 tangerines, juiced and zested
3 tbsp. extra virgin olive oil
2 tbsp. dry white wine
1 tsp. fresh rosemary
½ tsp. fresh thyme
¼ tsp. coarsely ground black pepper
Vegetable cooking spray
Fresh herbs, for garnish
Tangerine slices, for garnish

Place the fillets in a shallow dish. Combine the tangerine zest with tangerine juice, olive oil, white wine, herbs, and black pepper in a small bowl; mix well. Pour the marinade over the fish and marinate for 1 to 2 hours in refrigerator. Coat grill with vegetable spray and preheat on medium-high heat. Grill fillets for 4 to 5 minutes on each side until center is opaque and meat flakes easily with a fork. Garnish with herbs and tangerine slices and serves. Serves 4.

Orange-Baked Triggerfish

1 lb. triggerfish fillets, thawed if frozen
¼ cup cooking oil or butter, melted
3 tbsp. orange juice
4 tsp. grated orange peel
1 cup bacon-flavored crackers, finely crushed
1 tsp. paprika
½ tsp. seasoned salt
Orange slices, for garnish

Preheat oven to 450 degrees. Cut fillets into serving-size portions. Combine oil, orange juice, and orange peel. Mix crackers, paprika, and salt. Dip fish in oil mixture and roll in cracker mixture. Place fish in a single layer in a well-greased 1½–quart shallow casserole dish. Pour remaining oil mixture over the fish. Bake for 10 to 12 minutes or until fish flakes easily with a fork. Garnish with orange slices. Serves 4.

Potato-Crusted Trigger

2 lbs. triggerfish fillets, thawed if frozen
½ tsp. garlic salt
½ cup plus 2 tsp. instant mashed potato
    flakes, divided
Oil for frying
1 cup chicken broth
1 tbsp. chopped green onion
1 tbsp. chopped parsley

Cut triggerfish fillets into 6 portions. Sprinkle fish with garlic salt and roll in ½ cup mashed potato flakes. Place fish in a single layer into hot oil in a 10-inch frying pan. Fry at moderate heat for 4 to 5 minutes or until brown. Turn carefully. Fry 4 to 5 minutes longer or until fish are brown and flake easily with a fork. Drain on a paper towel. Keep warm. When all fish have been fried, add remaining ingredients to oil in pan. Simmer for 1 to 2 minutes or until thick, stirring constantly. Pour sauce over fish. Serves 6.

Potato-Crusted Trigger

Snappy Trigger

2 lbs. triggerfish fillets, thawed if frozen
½ cup frozen orange juice concentrate,
   thawed
¼ cup salad oil
¼ cup soy sauce
¼ cup cider vinegar
½ tsp. salt
Chopped parsley, for garnish

Cut fillets into six portions. Place fish in a single layer on a well-greased 15 x 10-inch baking pan. In a small dish, combine orange juice concentrate, salad oil, soy sauce, cider vinegar, and salt. Brush fish with sauce. Broil about 4 inches from heat source for 5 minutes. Turn fish carefully and brush with sauce. Broil 5 to 7 minutes longer or until lightly browned and fish flakes easily with a fork. Sprinkle with parsley. Serves 6.

Triggerfish Florentine

8 oz. triggerfish fillets, thawed if frozen
1 9-10-oz. package frozen creamed spinach,
   cooked according to package directions
2 tbsp. dry bread crumbs
¼ tsp. nutmeg
Dash pepper
2 tbsp. grated Parmesan cheese
Lemon wedges, for serving

Preheat oven to 350 degrees. Place triggerfish fillets in a well-greased 8 x 8-inch baking pan. In a separate dish, combine cooked spinach, bread crumbs, nutmeg, and pepper. Spread topping over fillets. Sprinkle with cheese. Bake for 20 to 25 minutes or until fillets flake easily with a fork. Serve with lemon wedges. Serves 2.

Tripletail

The tripletail gets its name from the arrangement of fins that sit far back on its body so that it appears that the fish has three tail fins. Some say that the tripletail—or blackfish, as it is known in some areas—has the look of a giant freshwater bream, if you can imagine a bream reaching twenty pounds.

These fish hang around piers, pilings and floating debris, where they lazily wait for a meal to swim by.

The flesh is excellent but, due to its flat shape, not plentiful in comparison to the fish's size.

Tripletail is not a common market species. It is most often brought to the table by fishermen.

Barbecued Tripletail

1½ lbs. tripletail fillets, thawed if frozen
⅓ cup Worcestershire sauce
1 cup ketchup
2 tbsp. butter
⅓ cup chopped onion
3 tbsp. white vinegar
2 tbsp. brown sugar
1 tbsp. prepared mustard

Cut tripletail into serving-size portions. In small a saucepan, mix remaining ingredients. Bring to a boil, reduce heat, and simmer for 10 minutes. Allow to cool. Arrange fish in a shallow baking dish and pour sauce over fish. Marinate for 30 minutes to 1 hour in refrigerator, turning once. Preheat oven to 350 degrees. Transfer fish to a well-greased baking dish and baste with remaining marinade. Bake for 20 to 25 minutes. Serves 4.

Country-Flavored Tripletail Soup

1 lb. tripletail fillets, thawed if frozen
2 tsp. butter, melted, or vegetable oil
2 tsp. flour
1½ tsp. instant minced onion
¾ tsp. salt
¼ tsp. white pepper
¼ tsp. ground nutmeg
1 cup half-and-half
1 8½-oz. can whole kernel corn, undrained
Chopped parsley, for garnish

Cut tripletail fillets into 1-inch pieces. In a 3-quart saucepan, combine butter, flour, onion, salt, pepper, and nutmeg. Gradually add half-and-half, stirring constantly. Add fish and corn. Cook over medium heat, stirring occasionally, for 8 to 10 minutes or until fish flakes easily with a fork. Garnish with chopped parsley. Serves 3.

Barbecued Tripletail

Poached Tripletail with Horseradish Sauce

8 oz. tripletail fillets, thawed if frozen
1½ cups water
1 tbsp. lemon juice
¼ tsp. salt
Paprika to taste
Horseradish sauce, for serving

Horseradish Sauce

¼ cup Miracle Whip
1 tbsp. horseradish
½ tsp. instant minced onion
⅛ tsp. paprika

Place fillets in an 8-inch frying pan. Add water, lemon juice, and salt. Cover and simmer for 5 to 10 minutes or until fish flakes easily with a fork. Remove fish to a hot platter. Sprinkle with paprika. Serve with horseradish sauce. Serves 2.

Combine all ingredients in a small bowl. Makes ¼ cup sauce.

Note: You can also substitute ⅛ cup mayonnaise and ⅛ cup sour cream for the Miracle Whip, if you prefer.

Tripletail and Broccoli

2 lbs. tripletail fillets, thawed if frozen
1 10-oz. package frozen chopped broccoli, cooked according to package directions
1 10¾-oz. can condensed cream of mushroom soup
½ cup processed cheese spread
2 tbsp. lemon juice
1 cup grated cheddar cheese

Preheat oven to 350 degrees. Place tripletail fillets in a well-greased 12 x 8-inch baking dish. Arrange broccoli on top of the fish. In a medium bowl, combine soup, cheese spread, and lemon juice. Pour over broccoli. Top with grated cheese. Bake for 30 to 35 minutes or until fish flakes easily with a fork. Serves 6.

Trout

Trout to bay fishermen are as import a part of sport fishing as mackerels are to summer gulf fishermen. By far, the most popular member of this family is the spotted seatrout, which can grow longer than two feet and reach more than fifteen pounds. On average, spotted seatrout are one to two feet long and weigh three to four pounds. The sand seatrout is a smaller and less-appreciated cousin, but it also makes a tasty meal, especially when prepared fresh.

The sand seatrout usually is not more than a foot long and a couple of pounds.

Both trouts have the same shape, but their coloring differs. The sand seatrout is silvery without strong markings, while the spotted seatrout has spots along its back and for the length of its body. Both are members of the drum family. Both are soft-fleshed fish, which means that they are excellent table fare when prepared fresh but not so much after having been frozen for any length of time.

They are available in fresh markets.

Country-Style Trout

Country Style Trout

2 lbs. trout fillets
¼ cup butter, softened
1 tbsp. minced shallots
1 clove garlic, minced
¼ tsp. pepper
⅛ tsp. lemon juice
1½ tbsp. finely chopped fresh parsley

Cut fish into 6 equal portions and set aside. In a small bowl, cream butter until smooth. Add shallots, garlic, pepper, and lemon juice; mix well. Add parsley; blend. Grease a broiler pan with non-stick cooking spray. Place fish on broiler pan and cover with butter mixture. Broil 3 to 4 inches from heat source for 5 minutes. Turn fish and baste with additional butter mixture and cook for an additional 3 to 5 minutes or until fish flakes easily with a fork. Serves 6.

Dill White Trout

2 lbs. pan-dressed trout, thawed if frozen
1½ tsp. salt
¼ tsp. pepper
½ cup butter
2 tsp. dill
3 tbsp. lemon juice

Cut fish lengthwise just enough so that both sides will lay flat, being careful not to cut all the way through. Spread open on a work surface. Sprinkle flesh with salt and pepper. Melt butter in a 10-inch frying pan. Add dill. Place fish in a single layer, flesh side down, in the hot dill butter. Fry over moderate heat for 2 to 3 minutes. Turn carefully. Fry 2 to 3 minutes longer or until fish flakes easily with a fork. Place fish on a warm serving platter and keep warm. When all fish have been fried, turn heat very low and stir lemon juice into remaining butter. Pour sauce over fish. Serves 6.

Fantastic Seatrout

1½ lbs. trout fillets, skinned and deboned, thawed if frozen
⅓ cup milk
2 tsp. lemon pepper, divided
2 tsp. Worcestershire sauce
1½ tbsp. dehydrated minced onion flakes
½ tsp. salt
½ tsp. basil
¼ tsp. dry mustard
¼ tsp. paprika

Preheat oven to 400 degrees. In a shallow dish, combine milk, 1½ tsp. lemon pepper, Worcestershire sauce, and onion flakes. Dip both sides of each trout fillet in milk mixture. Place fillets in a single layer in a 12 x 8-inch baking dish. Spoon any remaining milk mixture evenly over fish. Combine salt, remaining ½ tsp. lemon pepper, basil, dry mustard, and paprika; sprinkle over fillets. Bake for 10 to 15 minutes or until fish flakes easily with a fork. Serves 4.

Seatrout with Mushrooms

1 tsp. olive oil
1 clove garlic, crushed
4 oz. mushrooms, sliced
2 tbsp. light soy sauce
2 tbsp. sherry
1 lb. trout fillets

Heat olive oil over moderate heat. Add garlic and sauté until fragrant. Add mushrooms, soy sauce, and sherry. Move mushrooms to the edges of the skillet. Add trout fillets. Sauté briefly until fish flakes easily with a fork. Remove fillets to platter and top with mushrooms. Serves 3 to 4.

Trout Amandine

2 lbs. trout fillets, thawed if frozen
½ cup flour
1 tsp. seasoned salt
1 tsp. paprika
¼ cup butter, melted, divided
½ cup sliced almonds
2 tbsp. lemon juice
1 tbsp. chopped parsley
5 drops hot sauce

Cut fish into serving-size portions. Combine flour, seasoned salt, and paprika. Roll fish in flour mixture and place skin-side down in a 13 x 10-inch well-greased broiler pan. Drizzle 2 tbsp. butter over the fish. Broil approximately 4 inches from heat source for 8 to 10 minutes or until fish flakes easily with a fork. While fish is broiling, cook almonds in remaining 2 tbsp. butter until golden brown, stirring constantly. Remove from heat and stir in lemon juice, parsley, and hot sauce. Pour sauce over fish. Serve immediately. Serves 6.

Trout Thermidor

½ lb. trout fillets, thawed if frozen
2 tsp. butter
1 tsp. lemon juice
1 tbsp. flour
¼ tsp. salt
½ cup milk
1 tsp. chopped parsley
2 tbsp. grated Parmesan cheese
Paprika to taste

Preheat oven to 400 degrees. Cut trout fillets into bite-size pieces. Melt butter in an 8-inch frying pan. Add lemon juice and fish. Cook over low heat for 3 to 4 minutes, stirring frequently. Stir in flour and salt. Add milk gradually and cook until thick and smooth, stirring constantly. Add parsley. Place in 2 to 3 well-greased 6-oz. custard cups. Sprinkle with cheese and paprika. Bake for 10 to 12 minutes or until lightly browned. Serves 2.

Tuna

These fast, colorful, big fish are famous for their fighting ability and quality of flesh, which many enjoy cooked rare or medium rare. It has more similarities to red meat than most other fish. All of the tunas have a similar design: pointed like a bullet at both ends with a tailfin for propulsion. They are built for speed, and because of that are easily identified.

Blackfins are found nearest to shore and sometimes are caught by fishermen targeting king mackerel. A popular area for the yellowfin is around the oil rigs in deep water off the coasts of the western half of the northern gulf.

More and more fishermen are targeting the tunas as tighter limits are placed on snappers, groupers, amberjack, and triggerfish. Particularly popular in the northern gulf are the yellowfin tuna and its smaller cousin, the blackfin. Occasionally, a massive bluefin is brought in from local waters, but that species commands such a high price in Asian markets that it often is exported shortly after it hits the dock. Tunas are found at most markets.

Polynesian Yellowfin Tuna Steaks

2 lbs. yellowfin tuna steaks, thawed if frozen
⅓ cup soy sauce
1 8-oz. can unsweetened, crushed pineapple
2 tbsp. ketchup
2 tbsp. vegetable oil
2 tbsp. finely chopped parsley
1 tbsp. lemon juice
1 clove garlic, minced
½ tsp. oregano
½ tsp. pepper

Cut steaks into serving-size portions. Place fish in a single layer in a shallow dish. Combine all remaining ingredients. Pour sauce over fish and marinate in the refrigerator for 1 hour, turning once. Remove fish, reserving the marinade for basting, and place on a well-greased broiler pan. Broil about 4 inches from heat source for 3 to 4 minutes. Turn carefully and baste with marinade. Broil an additional 3 minutes or until tuna has a slightly pink center. Serves 6.

Note: Although this recipe calls for yellowfin tuna, any other tuna steak will be equally delicious!

Yellowfin Tuna with Pepper-Garlic Crust

4 8-oz. tuna steaks, 1½ inches thick
½ tbsp. salt
½ tbsp. crushed black peppercorns
1 tbsp. olive oil
1 clove garlic, chopped

Season the tuna steaks with salt and crushed black peppercorns. Heat oil in a skillet over high heat; add garlic and brown. Add tuna and sear to desired doneness, usually 2 minutes per side for a rare center, 5 to 8 minutes per side for a well-done center. Serves 4.

Seared Tuna

6 5-oz. tuna steaks
2 tbsp. olive oil
Salt and pepper to taste
1 cup chopped green onions, for garnish
1 lemon, quartered and seeded, for garnish

Place tuna on a plate. Coat tuna with olive oil and sprinkle with salt and pepper. Heat a heavy skillet over medium-high heat. Once the pan is very hot, sear tuna until medium rare, about 1 minute per side, and quickly remove from heat. Garnish with green onions and lemon. Serves 6.

Seared Tuna

Herb-Grilled Tuna

1½ lbs. tuna steaks
½ cup butter, melted
2 tbsp. lemon or lime juice
1 tsp. dill
½ tsp. basil
½ tsp. onion salt
¼ tsp. white pepper

Place steaks in a well-oiled, hinged wire grill. Combine remaining ingredients and use to baste fish. Cook about 4 inches from moderately hot coals for 5 to 6 minutes. Turn fish, baste with remaining butter mixture, and cook 4 to 5 minutes longer or until tuna has a slightly pink center. Serves 4.

Jiffy Broiled Tuna

6 tuna steaks, thawed if frozen
2 tbsp. vegetable oil
2 tbsp. soy sauce
2 tbsp. Worcestershire sauce
1 tsp. paprika
½ tsp. chili powder
½ tsp. garlic powder
⅛ tsp. hot sauce
Lemon wedges, for garnish

Place steaks in single layer on a well-greased broiler pan. Combine vegetable oil, soy sauce, Worcestershire sauce, paprika, chili powder, garlic powder, and hot sauce in a small bowl. Pour sauce over steaks, reserving some to baste. Broil tuna about 4 inches from heat source for 3 to 4 minutes. Turn carefully and baste with reserved sauce. Broil for 3 to 4 additional minutes or until tuna has a slightly pink center. Serves 6.

Tuna Buttermilk Bites

2 lbs. skinless tuna steaks, thawed if frozen
1 cup buttermilk
1 cup biscuit mix
1 tsp. salt
Cooking oil for deep frying

Cut steaks into bite-size pieces. Place in single layer in a shallow dish. Pour buttermilk over fish and let stand 30 minutes, turning once. In a separate dish, combine biscuit mix and salt. Remove fish from buttermilk and roll in biscuit mix. Fry in oil heated to approximately 350 degrees for 3 to 5 minutes or until fish is brown and flakes easily with a fork. Drain on absorbent paper. Place toothpicks in fish bites and serve with a favorite seafood sauce. Serves 12 as an appetizer.

Wahoo

Hooking a wahoo is like hooking a bullet fired from a gun, except for two things: first, the wahoo may seem faster than the bullet, and, second, the wahoo can abruptly change direction.

The wahoo flesh is much whiter than that of the king mackerel and is a far superior food fish to other mackerels found in the northern gulf.

The casual angler may mistake the wahoo—which can exceed two hundred pounds—for a king mackerel on steroids, but the wahoo is easily distinguished by its longer snout and the vertical bars along its sides. Usually (but not always) the Wahoo is caught a little farther offshore than the king mackerel and can chase down a bait with greater speed.

Wahoo can be found in many fresh markets during spring, summer, and fall months.

Pan-Seared Wahoo

4 tsp. olive oil, divided
½ cup chopped celery
3 green onions, chopped
1 tbsp. minced parsley, plus additional for
    garnish
2 wahoo fillets
Salt and pepper to taste
1 clove garlic, minced
Red pepper flakes to taste
2 tbsp. lime juice

Heat 2 tbsp. oil in a frying pan. Add celery, green onions, and parsley and sauté until soft. Remove to bowl and keep warm. Lightly salt and pepper fillets. Add remaining 2 tbsp. olive oil to pan, bring to medium-high heat, and place fillets in pan. Cook fillets for 5 minutes. Turn and cook for 4 minutes. Add garlic and red pepper flakes to pan. Cook until garlic becomes fragrant, then add fresh lime juice. Return cooked celery, onions, and parsley to frying pan, covering the fillets. When heated through, serve immediately, adding additional parsley as a garnish. Serves 2.

Baked Wahoo with Panko

2 lbs. wahoo fillets
Salt and pepper to taste
1 large egg
2 tbsp. milk
1 cup flour
Panko bread crumbs
Vegetable oil
¼ cup butter

Preheat oven to 350 degrees. Sprinkle wahoo fillets with salt and pepper. In a shallow dish, mix egg and milk to create a wash. Place flour in a second bowl and panko in a third bowl. Coat fillets in egg wash, then dredge in flour and shake off any excess. Roll coated fish in panko, pressing each fillet firmly to achieve a thorough coating. Grease a baking dish large enough to hold fish in a single layer with vegetable oil. Place fillets in the dish and top each fillet with a pat of butter. Bake for 20 minutes. Remove from oven, turn fillets over, increase oven to 375 degrees, and return fillets to the oven for 5 minutes. Remove from oven, turn fillets again, and increase oven to 400 degrees. Remove fish when it is browned and flakes easily with a fork. Serves 6 to 8.

Pan-Seared Wahoo

Grilled Wahoo

1 tbsp. olive oil
1 tbsp. lemon juice
1 tbsp. paprika
1 tsp. crushed red pepper flakes
4 5-oz. wahoo steaks

Combine the olive oil, lemon juice, paprika, and red pepper. Place wahoo steaks in a dish and pour the olive oil mixture over the fish. Marinate in refrigerator for at least half an hour. Remove fish from refrigerator, and cook on a charcoal grill for 15 minutes, turning once halfway through and basting fish with remaining marinade. Grill until fillets flake easily with a fork. Serves 4.

Whiting

Also known as gulf kingfish, the whiting of the northern gulf is a superior food fish, equally delicious fried or broiled. This member of the croaker family and its close cousin, the southern kingfish or ground mullet, can be identified by the single barbel on the chin. Both fish look remarkably similar in shape, but the whiting is silvery while the ground mullet has a brownish-gray cast.

Whiting is an excellent target for a fishing outing because they can be caught with the most basic of fishing gear and such economic bait as peeled bits of dead shrimp. Whiting is almost always caught in the surf and grows to about one foot in length. A whopper can reach a foot and a half or more.

Fresh whiting can be found in many fresh markets throughout the region. In addition, frozen whiting is available in most grocery stores.

Broiled Pan-Dressed Whiting

3 lbs. pan-dressed whiting, thawed if frozen
¼ cup butter, melted
¼ cup lemon juice
1½ tsp salt
⅛ tsp. pepper
¾ tsp. paprika

Clean fish thoroughly and dry. Place fish on a well-greased 13 x 10-inch broiler pan. Thoroughly combine remaining ingredients. Brush fish inside and out with butter mixture, reserving some for basting. Broil fish approximately 4 inches from heat source for 5 to 8 minutes. Turn carefully and baste with sauce. Broil for 5 to 8 additional minutes or until fish flakes easily with a fork. Serves 6.

Whiting with Vegetable Medley

4 5-6-oz. whiting fillets
4 tbsp. olive oil, divided
1 cup diced eggplant
1 cup diced onion
1 cup diced red bell pepper
1 cup diced green bell pepper
1 cup diced zucchini
½ tsp. dried oregano
1 tsp. minced garlic
½ tsp. salt
½ tsp. ground pepper

Preheat grill or broiler. Brush whiting with 1 tbsp. olive oil. Grill or broil for about 4 minutes or until it flakes easily. In a non-stick skillet, heat 1 tbsp. olive oil. Add eggplant, sauté for 2 minutes, and remove with a slotted spoon to a dish. Add remaining 2 tbsp. olive oil to skillet. Add onion and red and green pepper and sauté for 1½ minutes. Add zucchini; sauté for 1½ minutes. Add oregano, garlic, salt, and pepper, and sauté for 1 minute. Return eggplant to the pan and heat through. Serve with whiting. Serves 4.

Crunchy Baked Whiting

2 lbs. whiting fillets
1 cup light mayonnaise
1 cup sour cream
2 tbsp. ranch-style salad dressing mix
¼ cup finely chopped green onion
3 tbsp. lime juice
2 3-oz. cans French-fried onion rings, crushed

Preheat oven to 375 degrees. Spray a shallow baking dish with non-stick cooking spray. Place whiting fillets in the dish in a single layer. Blend mayonnaise, sour cream, salad dressing mix, green onion, and lime juice; pour over fish. Cover with crushed onion rings. Bake for 20 minutes or until fish flakes easily with a fork. Serves 6.

Lemon-Herb Baked Whiting

4 6-oz. whiting fillets
2 tbsp. olive oil
3 tbsp. lemon juice
½ tsp. chopped fresh basil
1 tsp. chopped fresh rosemary
1 tsp. chopped fresh thyme
½ medium onion, thinly sliced
½ medium red bell pepper, diced
Salt and pepper to taste
1 lemon, sliced
½ cup dry white wine
2 tbsp. chopped parsley

Preheat oven to 350 degrees. Place fillets in a single layer on a greased baking dish. Drizzle olive oil and lemon juice over whiting fillets. Season fish with basil, rosemary, thyme, onion, bell pepper, salt, and pepper. Top with lemon slices and white wine. Bake for 25 to 30 minutes or until fish flakes easily with a fork. Sprinkle with chopped parsley and serve. Serves 4.

Pan-Fried Whiting

⅔ cup cornmeal
½ tsp. salt
½ tsp. paprika
2 lbs. whiting fillets
Vegetable oil, for frying

Combine corn meal, salt, and paprika in a shallow dish. Coat fillets with cornmeal mixture. Pour approximately ⅛ inch oil in a heavy skillet and heat to 360 degrees. Place fillets in skillet and fry for 4 to 5 minutes or until brown. Turn carefully and cook an additional 4 to 5 minutes or until fish flakes easily with a fork. Drain excess oil on a paper towel. Serves 6.

Index

almaco jack, 79
amberjack, 31, 79-80, 82-84, 179
Amberjack St. Augustine, 82
Amberjack with Spanish Rice, 82
Apricot-Glazed Swordfish, 158

Bacon-Baked Oysters, 51
Baked King Mackerel Steaks, 128
Baked Shark with Mushrooms, 141
Baked Stuffed Snapper Fillets, 151
Baked Triggerfish with Vegetables, 166
Baked Wahoo with Panko, 184
banded rudderfish, 79
Barbecued Tripletail, 172
Batter-Fried Shark, 141
Batter-Fried Triggerfish, 166
black drum, 100, 109-10
Blackened Redfish, 112
blackfish. *See* tripletail
black sea bass, 85-86, 88
Black Sea Bass Supreme, 86
Blount County Fried Fish, 88
blue crab, 39-42, 44
Blue Crab Imperial, 41
Blue Crab Stuffing, 41, 117
bluefish, 89-90, 92
Bluefish and Onions, 92
Bluefish Salad Supreme, 90
Boiled Blue Crab, 42
Boiled Lobster, 48
Boiled Shrimp, 67
Broiled Dolphin with Tangy Glaze, 105
Broiled Drum, 110
Broiled Pan-Dressed Whiting, 188
Broiled Rock Shrimp, 56
Broiled Scallops, 62
Broiled Shark with Orange Butter, 144
Broiled Sheepshead, 146
butchering, 25, 27
butterfly fillets, 25-26, 32
Buttery Baked Grouper, 122

Captain's Choice, 127

catfish, 94-95
Cheese-Crusted Amberjack, 83
Chipper Croaker, 101
Chorizo- and Crab-Stuffed Grouper, 121
cobia, 96-98
Cobia in Wine Sauce, 97
cooked seafood, 22
Country-Flavored Tripletail Soup, 172
Country-Style Trout, 177
crab, 20
Crab Cakes, 42
Crab-Stuffed Flounder, 117
Creamy Orzo with Scallops, Asparagus, and
    Parmesan, 60
croaker, 100-102, 109, 187
Croaker Stir-Fry, 101
Crunchy Baked Whiting, 190
Crusty Lobster Turnovers, 46
cusk eel, 104
cutting board, 27

Deviled Crab, 44
Deviled Rock Shrimp, 56
Dill White Trout, 177
dolphin, 104-6, 108
drawn fish, 25
dressed fish, 25-26, 28
drum, 109-10, 114, 176

Easy Triggerfish and Broccoli Casserole, 167
Emerald Coast Snapper, 151

Fantastic Seatrout, 177
Fast Catfish Broil, 94
fatty fish, 17
Festive Bluefish, 92
fillets, 25-26, 30
Flash-in-the-Pan Flounder, 116
Florida Pompano Amandine, 138
Florida Red Snapper, 154
flounder, 115-18
Flounder Amandine, 116
Flounder Casserole, 118

Flounder Mushroom Medley, 118
Flounder with Citrus Marinade, 117
fresh fish, 17, 20-21
fresh shellfish, 21
Fried Grouper Sandwich, 122
Fried Oysters, 51
Fried Scallops, 60
Fried Squid, 76
frozen fish, 19, 21-22
frozen shellfish, 22

gafftopsail catfish, 93-95
Gafftopsail Catfish in Cream, 95
Ginger-Honey Drum, 110
gray snapper, 150
Grayton Beach Grouper Soup, 121
Great Gulf Redfish Chowder, 112
Greek Catfish, 95
Greek Cobia Fillets, 98
green shrimp, 64
Grilled Amberjack, 80
Grilled Amberjack with Artichoke Mushroom
    Sauce, 80
Grilled Bluefish, 90
Grilled Bluefish with Fresh Corn Salsa, 92
Grilled Cobia Steaks, 98
Grilled Mahi-Mahi with Lime, 105
Grilled Redfish, 111
Grilled Spanish Mackerel, 127
Grilled Swordfish, 160
Grilled Triggerfish Tangerine, 167
Grilled Wahoo, 186
ground mullet, 187
grouper, 88-89, 104, 120-22, 124-25, 179
Grouper Creole, 125
Grouper Encrusted with Caramelized Onions,
    124
Grouper Kiev, 124
Grouper Mediterranean, 125
Grouper Parmesan, 125
Guacamole, 106
gulf cod, 104
gulf kingfish, 100, 187

Heavenly Catfish, 95
Herb-Broiled Mackerel Steaks, 127
Herbed Croaker 'n Chips, 102
Herb-Grilled Tuna, 182
Herb-Roasted Tilefish, 162
Herb-Seasoned Cobia Steaks, 98
Honey-Broiled Scallops, 62
Horseradish-Crusted Snapper, 154
Horseradish Sauce, 174
Hot Honey Amberjack, 83

Italian-Style Redfish, 114

Jambalaya, 68
Jiffy Broiled Tuna, 182
Just Delicious Fish, 88

Kiev-Style Pompano, 137
king mackerel, 126, 128, 130, 179, 183
knife, 27

lane snapper, 150, 155
lean fish, 17
Lemon Butter, 56
Lemon-Herb Baked Whiting, 190
Lemon Pepper Amberjack, 84
lesser amberjack, 79
Lime-Grilled Cobia, 97
lobster, 20, 39-40, 45-46, 48, 55, 64

mackerel, 126-28, 130
Mahi-Mahi à la Pepper, 108
Mahi-Mahi Pontchartrain, 108
mahi-mahi. *See* dolphin
Marler Fish Cakes, 130
marlin, 104
Microwave Fine Fish, 88
mullet, 100, 131, 133-35, 187
Mullet Casserole Panacea, 134
Mullet in Coral Sauce, 134
Mullet Shoestring Casserole, 133
Mushroom-Walnut Sauce, 148

Natalie's Crab Dip, 44

Old-Fashioned Buttermilk Catfish, 94
Onion-Baked Mullet, 133
Orange-Baked Triggerfish, 168
Oriental Amberjack Steaks, 84
Oven-Fried Redfish, 111
oysters, 19-20, 49, 51, 53-54
Oysters en Creole Sauce, 54
Oysters on the Grill, 54

Oysters Rockefeller, 53

Pan-Fried White Snapper, 152
Pan-Fried Whiting, 190
Pan-Grilled Snapper with Avocado-Strawberry
    Salsa, 152
Pan-Seared Mahi-Mahi Tacos with Guacamole
    and Pico de Gallo, 106
Pan-Seared Wahoo, 184
Pico de Gallo, 106
Poached Tripletail with Horseradish Sauce, 174
Polynesian Yellowfin Tuna Steaks, 180
pompano, 136-38, 144
Pompano in Foil, 137
Pompano with Tomatoes, 138
porgy. *See* white snapper
Potato-Crusted Trigger, 168

Quick Croaker, 102

red drum. *See* redfish
redfish, 109-12, 114
red snapper, 150, 154-55, 165
Roasted Greek Shrimp with Orzo, 71
rock shrimp, 55-58, 64
Rock Shrimp Dreams, 57
Rock Shrimp Étouffée, 57
Rock Shrimp Stir-Fry with Crunchy Vegetables, 58
Rock Shrimp with Linguine, 58

sand seatrout, 176
Sautéed Scallops, 62
Savory Baked Drum, 114
Scalloped Oysters, 53
Scallop Gazpacho, 63
scallops, 20, 59-60, 62-63
Scallops with Peaches, 63
Scrumptious Broiled Snapper, 155
Seafood Marinara with Pasta, 76
Seared Tuna, 180
Seatrout with Mushrooms, 178
Sesame Dolphin Bites, 105
Sesame Grilled Black Sea Bass, 86
shark, 140-41, 143-44
Shark en Papillote, 144
Shark in Tomato and Citrus Sauce, 143
Shark Italiano, 143
sheepshead, 145-46, 148-49
Sheepshead Chowder, 146
Sheepshead Fillets and Wild Rice, 148
Sheepshead Macadamia, 149
Sheepshead Onion Bake, 149
shovelnose lobster, 45

shrimp, 19, 23, 39, 55, 64-69, 71-73
Shrimp and Grits, 72
Shrimp Cocktail Sauce, 66
Shrimp Creole, 66
Shrimp Kabobs, 67
Shrimp Pilau, 69
Shrimp Scampi, 71
Smoked Mullet, 135
Smoky Mullet Salad, 135
snapper, 88-89, 150-52, 154-56, 179
Snapper Boca Chica, 155
Snapper Scampi, 156
Snappy Trigger, 170
southern kingfish, 100, 187
Southern Soft-Shell Crab Amandine, 44
Spanish mackerel, 126-27
spiny lobster, 45
spotted seatrout, 176
squid, 74-76
Squid in Tomato Sauce, 75
steaks, 25-26, 29
stone crab, 40
Stuffed Shrimp, 69
Sunshine Snapper, 156
swordfish, 157-58, 160

Tangy King Mackerel Steaks, 128
Teriyaki Swordfish, 158
tilefish, 161-62, 164
Tilefish Excelsior, 164
Tilefish Torney, 164
triggerfish, 31, 165-68, 167, 170, 179
Triggerfish Florentine, 170
tripletail, 171-72, 174-75
Tripletail and Broccoli, 175
trout, 109, 176-78
Trout Amandine, 178
Trout Thermidor, 178
tuna, 179-80, 182
Tuna Buttermilk Bites, 182

vermilion snapper, 150, 155

wahoo, 183-84, 186
Western-Style Croaker, 101
West Indies Salad, 42
white snapper, 150, 152
whiting, 100, 109, 187-88, 190
Whiting with Vegetable Medley, 188
whole fish, 25

Yellowfin Tuna with Pepper-Garlic Crust, 180